STUDENT UNIT GUIDE

NEW EDITION

OCR A2 Psychology Unit G544

Approaches and Research Methods in Psychology

David Clarke

 PHILIP ALLAN

Philip Allan, an imprint of Hodder Education, part of Hachette UK, Market Place, Deddington, Oxfordshire OX15 0SE

Orders
Bookpoint Ltd, 130 Milton Park, Abingdon, Oxfordshire OX14 4SB
tel: 01235 827827
fax: 01235 400401
e-mail: education@bookpoint.co.uk
Lines are open 9.00 a.m.–5.00 p.m., Monday to Saturday, with a 24-hour message answering service.
You can also order through the Philip Allan Updates website: www.philipallan.co.uk

© David Clarke 2012

ISBN 978-1-4441-6245-5

First printed 2012
Impression number 5 4 3 2 1
Year 2017 2016 2015 2014 2013 2012

Cover photo: Fotolia

Printed in Dubai

Typeset by Integra, India

Hachette UK's policy is to use papers that are natural, renewable and recyclable products and made from wood grown in sustainable forests. The logging and manufacturing processes are expected to conform to the environmental regulations of the country of origin.

P02023

Contents

Content Guidance

Questions & Answers

Getting the most from this book

Questions & Answers

Exam-style questions

Examiner comments on the questions
Tips on what you need to do to gain full marks, indicated by the icon **e**.

Sample student answers
Practise the questions, then look at the student answers that follow each set of questions.

Examiner commentary on sample student answers
Find out how many marks each answer would be awarded in the exam and then read the examiner comments (preceded by the icon **e**) following each student answer. Annotations that link back to points made in the student answers show exactly how and where marks are gained or lost.

Section **A**

(6) Briefly discuss the validity of your study. (3 marks)

You know about validity is (and hopefully you haven't confused it with reliability), so what about your study: is it measuring what it claims to measure?

(7) Outline one way in which you show awareness of ethical issues in the conduct of your study. (3 marks)

The easiest way to show that any study you have done is ethical is to have a sentence or two on standardised instructions. This means that at the outset you ask your participants 'Do you give your consent to take part?' If you have the additional comment 'You have the right to withdraw at any time', you have met two ethical guidelines.

Student A

(1) There will be a significant difference **a** in the rates of deception **b** between males and females **c**.

2/3 marks awarded The student has a hypothesis (correctly) rather than a null hypothesis. There is inclusion of a 'significant difference' and there is the inclusion of some form of **b** DV and **d** IV. However, it is not clear what is meant by 'rates of deception' — it is not precise enough.

(2) I will use a survey to investigate this. I will ask 20 males and 20 females from around my college to take part, so it will be an opportunity sample and the parent population **a** will be college students between 16 and 19 years of age. The questionnaire **b** will ask them questions such as:

What is your sex?
Has anyone deceived you in the last 6 months?
If yes, please give brief details of each occasion, e.g. relationship of person to you and what they deceived you about:
Occasion 1:
Person: relationship to you _____ male / female _____
What they deceived you about:
Occasion 2:
Person: relationship to you _____ male / female _____
What they deceived you about:
Occasion 3:
Etc. (as above — there will be room to write about up to 10 occasions)
I will approach each possible participant. I will give them a brief outline of the study and tell them it is about being deceived. Then I will ask them if they consent to participate. If they do, I will tell them that they will have the right to withdraw and that they can decide to stop participating at any time. I will also tell them that all of the contents of their questionnaire will be completely anonymous and I will not share them with anybody. I will give them the questionnaire to fill in themselves and an envelope in which to return it to me. I will then analyse the results by making a note of the deceptions and who deceived whom etc.

Unit G544: Approaches and Research Methods in Psychology 71

About this book

This book is a guide to **Approaches and Research Methods in Psychology**, compulsory **Unit G544** of the A2 specification (aggregation code H568). This A2 unit may be referred to as 'the synoptic unit'. This means that it is designed to test the knowledge, understanding and skills you have gained from the other AS and A2 psychology units and your ability to make links across different areas in answering questions. This unit guide is not a textbook; it is an aid to help you through the course and your revision. The emphasis is on informing you about exactly what you need to do and what you need to know to be successful in the examinations.

This guide has two sections:
- **Content Guidance.** This takes you through the material that you need to cover for the examinations. It is divided into two main parts: the first part covers various aspects of research methods in psychology, while the second part covers a range of approaches, perspectives, debates and issues that are important in psychology. Many marks can be gained from a simple evaluation strategy. The Content Guidance section helps you to develop your own evaluative skills, and therefore to get a better grade.
- **Questions & Answers.** The final section of the book provides sample examination questions and answers that are followed by examiner's comments and marks. The answers provided here are not intended to be model answers, so do not learn them and try to reproduce them in your own examination. The best thing to do is to look at the responses and the comments of the examiner, and then try to apply the best techniques to your own answers. You might find it useful to attempt your own answers to the specimen questions before you read the examiner's comments.

The specification

Skills from AS

Unit G544 builds on the work you have done in the AS part of the course and the A2 options in a number of ways:
- It considers how the five core approaches of psychology (cognitive, developmental, social, physiological and individual differences) apply in a variety of real-world contexts.
- It brings together the range of methods and techniques covered at AS (self-report, experiments, observations and correlation) and considers how these are used in each of the A2 options.
- It brings together methodological issues (such as reliability and validity), sampling techniques, experimental designs and data analysis techniques, and considers these in relation to each of the A2 options.
- It brings together psychological issues, debates and perspectives raised at AS (such as ethics, ecological validity, quantitative and qualitative data, and snapshot and longitudinal studies), showing their relevance to each of the A2 options.

New skills for A2

The A2 course introduces a number of new debates which are not covered at AS:

- determinism and free will
- reductionism and holism
- nature–nurture
- ethnocentrism
- psychology as science
- individual and situational explanations
- the usefulness of psychological research

The purpose of the options units is to apply approaches, methods and issues to specific subject matter, namely that from forensics, health, sport and education. The purpose of this compulsory synoptic unit is to bring together approaches, methods and issues covered elsewhere in the specification and add to them, extending knowledge and understanding.

Background

The fundamental questions of psychology are:

- Why do people behave like this?
- Why do people feel like this?
- Why do people think like this?

This unit is designed to encourage you to think about these questions in two main ways:

- how you might set about discovering the answers by planning a research project
- the different types of explanations or answers that psychology has generated from the different approaches and perspectives

In many ways, the content of this unit is central to the study of psychology. If you go on to study psychology at university, you may or may not encounter some of the core studies from your AS course. However, you will certainly have to study research methods again, as well as the various approaches, perspectives, issues and debates — and in more depth and detail.

Section A: Research methods in psychology

Section A of the specification for this unit focuses on research methods, including the design of a research project. This section draws heavily on the material you learnt for Unit G541, Psychological Investigations. However, the emphasis here is rather different: you have to *design* a study in order to investigate a particular idea or research aim. You will need to use all your knowledge about experiments, self-report, observations and correlations, sampling, ethics, experimental designs and so on. You should design a study which, if you wanted or needed to, you could actually carry out yourself. Therefore, you should bear practical considerations in mind. You need knowledge and experience of:

- the selection of a research question
- the choice of an appropriate method (e.g. experiment, self-report, questionnaire, correlation)

- the framing of operationalised hypotheses, including null and research hypotheses, and one- and two-tailed hypotheses
- the description and justification of the chosen design, whether it be independent samples, repeated measures or matched pairs
- populations, a suitable sample and sampling methods or techniques used to select participants
- materials used in conducting a study
- the procedure, including the measurement of variables, recorded using observations, self-reports or tests that generate nominal or at least ordinal data
- the control of extraneous variables, such as participant, experimenter and situational variables
- the counterbalancing of conditions (if appropriate) and the allocation of participants to groups
- the consideration of ethical issues that are applicable to the study
- the levels of measurement of the data (nominal, ordinal and possibly interval data)
- the collection and recording of data
- the presentation of the data, including descriptive statistics, measures of central tendency and dispersion (e.g. range), data tables and graphs
- the analysis of data (using inferential statistics): nonparametric tests (sign test, chi-square, Wilcoxon, Mann–Whitney, Spearman) and levels of significance (probability, avoiding type 1 and type 2 errors)

In addition, you must consider:
- the strengths and weaknesses of different research methods
- the strengths and weaknesses of any aspect of the design, and the validity and reliability of the measurements
- the ethics of any procedure
- possible future research that could be conducted
- alternative designs and samples

Section B: Approaches, perspectives, methods, issues and debates

Section B of the specification for this unit involves structured synoptic questions focusing on approaches, perspectives, methods, issues and debates. It examines all the key themes you have come across in all of your other units. For example, when studying for G542 (Core Studies), you will have come across the physiological approach, the cognitive approach and so on. You may well have come across these again later in your A2 applied psychology options for G543: for example, if you studied forensic psychology, you would probably have touched on the cognitive approach when you studied criminal thinking patterns. In a way, there is nothing completely new in this unit in terms of knowledge. What *is* new is that now the focus is on these approaches, perspectives etc. and on applying them and drawing knowledge together.

There are five core *approaches* of psychology that you need to know and understand:
- cognitive
- physiological
- individual differences

- developmental
- social

There are two *perspectives*:
- behaviourist
- psychodynamic

There are a number of topics concerning *methods*:
- experiment
- self-report
- correlation
- observation
- case study
- methodological issues such as reliability and validity

There are also a number of *issues* and *debates*:
- ethics
- ecological validity
- longitudinal and snapshot studies
- qualitative data and quantitative data
- determinism and free will
- reductionism and holism
- nature–nurture
- ethnocentrism
- psychology as science
- individual and situational explanations
- the usefulness of psychological research

Content Guidance

Research methods in psychology

Research methods

There are five main research methods: experiment, self-report, correlation, observation and case study. This section will describe each in turn, before summarising their strengths and weaknesses.

Experiment

One of the ideas behind the experimental method is that of cause and effect — that changes or differences in one thing bring about changes in another. For example, if you drink a large quantity of caffeinated coffee, you may start to feel jittery and shaky. Here the cause is coffee or caffeine, and the effect is feeling jittery and shaky. In experimental methods, the independent variable (IV) is the thing which is thought to be the cause, and the dependent variable (DV) is the effect. The following example shows how the relationship between caffeine and shakiness might be investigated by an experiment (though, please note, it would not be ethical).

An **experiment** is where the independent variable (IV) is the thing which is thought to be the cause, and the dependent variable (DV) is the effect.

Examiner tip
Many students get the IV and DV the wrong way around. Make sure you do not!

STUDY A, Experiment 1: the caffeine and shakiness experiment

I could find a sample of people and randomly allocate them to two different groups. One group drinks herbal tea (no caffeine group) and the other drinks strong caffeinated coffee (caffeine group). I could then measure their jitteriness by asking them to hold out their hands as still as possible and rating them for their stillness versus shakiness on a 10-point scale, where 1 = absolutely still and 10 = extremely shaky.

Here, we can see that:
- type of drink (caffeinated or not caffeinated) = the IV (the cause)
- shakiness (as measured by rating hand stillness/shakiness) = the DV (the effect)

The different kinds of experiment

There are three different kinds of experiment: laboratory experiment, field experiment and natural (or quasi-) experiment.

In a laboratory or field experiment, the researcher manipulates the IV. That is, the researcher *makes* the conditions happen or decides who is in which group. The researcher can then measure the effects (the DV). In a natural experiment, the IV varies naturally, without the researcher's intervention. The researcher will have some way of knowing which group or condition the person is in and will then simply measure the effects.

A laboratory experiment takes place in a laboratory or under 'controlled conditions'. It does not happen in a normal environment for the participant. A field experiment happens in 'the field': that is, in a natural or *normal* place — the sort of place you would expect to find people doing whatever it is that you are interested in as a researcher. A natural experiment can happen anywhere — laboratory (controlled conditions) or field (normal place). The important thing is that there is an IV, but it is one which varies or occurs naturally and the researcher has not intervened in order to vary it. The three different kinds of experiment are described in more detail below.

> **Knowledge check 1**
>
> Give one similarity and one difference between a laboratory experiment and a field experiment.

The laboratory experiment

Many people view the laboratory experiment as the main sort of experiment. We already know:
- It happens in controlled conditions.
- The researcher manipulates the IV.

'Controlled conditions' means somewhere that is kept the same for all participants and that is not where you would naturally come across the particular behaviour you are investigating. It could be a laboratory, a clinical room, or someone's office borrowed as a quiet place to conduct your experiment. For Experiment 1 (see page 9), you could use a classroom at lunchtime. It would be a 'controlled environment' so long as it is quiet, no one else is around, and so on.

The researcher manipulates the IV. This means that the researcher decides, for Experiment 1, who gets the caffeine and who does not, and also *how much* caffeine the participants have.

Two other examples of possible laboratory experiments are given below.

> **Examiner tip**
>
> It is crucial that you are able to identify the IV and DV correctly. This is why there are three examples of experiments here, all with the IV and DV clearly identified.

STUDY B, Experiment 2: colour of room and choice of music

I want to find out whether the colour of a room influences participants' choice of music. I find two rooms, and paint one a bright canary yellow and the other one a deep, moody blue. Participants are randomly allocated to either the 'yellow' condition or the 'blue' condition. They are asked to walk into the room and then to choose a track to listen to on an iPod while they do a simple crossword. The iPod has a choice of just four tracks: one each of drum and bass, soul, jazz and bhangra. I note which track they choose.
- IV = colour of room participant is placed in
- DV = choice of music

STUDY C, Experiment 3: doing homework with or without television on

Many students do their homework in front of the television. We want to find out whether watching television has any effect on task performance. Participants are asked to complete a moderately difficult crossword and then a set of simple sums on a 'brain training' program. They are timed and scored. Half an hour later, they are given another crossword and set of sums, but this time the television is switched on. Again they are timed and scored at these tasks.

- IV = television or no television
- DV = task performance on crossword and simple sums

The field experiment

A field experiment takes place in a natural or normal environment for the behaviour under scrutiny. For example, if you want to conduct a field experiment about how children learn you would base your study in a classroom. If you are interested in whether athletes improve their performance when there is an audience compared with when there is no audience, you would hold your experiment at the race track. Again, for it to be a real field experiment, the researcher has to manipulate or set up the different conditions of the IV. Two examples of possible field experiments follow.

STUDY D, Experiment 4: feedback on essays and student progress

Researchers are interested in how feedback to students on essays affects their progress and attainment in writing essays. In one class, half the students receive one type of feedback on their homework (feedback A) and the other half get another type of feedback (feedback B). Feedback A consists of giving a mark and an overall comment at the end of the essay (holistic). Feedback B consists of giving small comments throughout the work — on parts which are good, how some parts could be improved etc. — as well as an overall mark. This pattern of feedback continues for one term and all essay scores are noted.

- IV = type of feedback received
- DV = students' progress and attainment

STUDY E, Experiment 5: fashion magazines and effects on self-esteem

Researchers are interested in whether reading women's fashion and celebrity magazines, such as *Cosmopolitan* or *Hello!*, has an effect on self-esteem. Researchers think that looking at a fashion magazine might make the readers feel insecure about how they look (e.g. how they do their make-up, how their hair is cut, the shape of their bodies, the style of their clothes).

Customers arrive at a hairdresser's shop and are asked to wait for 5 minutes. Some participants are given a fashion magazine to read. Other participants are given a different type of magazine, about houses and gardens and recipes.

Knowledge check 2

What are 'controlled conditions'? Give an example of a 'controlled condition'.

Knowledge check 3

Give five examples of core studies that were done in a laboratory.

Examiner tip

There are an IV and a DV for all field experiments. An experiment has an IV and a DV whether it is conducted in or outside a laboratory.

Later, when each participant is seated in the hairdressing chair, the hairdresser asks, 'Are you happy with how you look at the moment?' The participants' replies are noted and later scored for how positive or negative their self-esteem is according to this response.

- IV = type of magazine
- DV = self-esteem score based upon response to question

The natural experiment

A natural experiment is one where the conditions of the IV happen by themselves. For example, we might be interested in whether males or females are more likely to do well on a memory test. The IV is sex — male or female. This cannot be 'manipulated' by the experimenter — it happens independently. Some other examples follow:

- Does age affect whether or not you follow the advice from a doctor? (The IV, age, is naturally occurring.)
- Does the weather affect whether people are more likely to return a greeting from a stranger? (The IV, the weather, is naturally occurring.)
- Do children who are born in months later in the school year (July, August) do less well at school than children who are born earlier in the school year (September, October)? (The IV, month of birth, happens naturally.)
- Are babies who are delivered by Caesarean section, rather than naturally, better or worse at dealing with stress? (This IV, type of birth, cannot be manipulated by the researcher for ethical reasons.)

We will come back to experiments later because much of the specification content regarding controls, designs, procedures and so on relates to experiments.

Self-report

Self-report simply means asking participants about something so they can report on it themselves. There are various ways of asking participants questions:

(1) Interview (face to face)
- **(a)** Structured interview: each participant is asked exactly the same questions in the same order.
- **(b)** Unstructured interview: the researcher asks different questions, depending on where the discussion takes him or her.
- **(c)** Semi-structured interview: the researcher has a certain number of set questions but can also ask other questions depending on where the responses take him or her, in order to investigate in more depth and prompt more detailed response.

(2) Questionnaires (paper or online): usually participants fill them in themselves.

Self-reports are useful for investigating things that would otherwise be difficult or impossible to measure or observe. For example, if a researcher wants to find out what people dream about every night, or, perhaps more interestingly, what people choose to think about as they are dropping off to sleep at night, there is no other way than to ask them. Self-report is also interesting for some of the *why* questions (e.g. Why do you play the lottery? Why do you smoke cigarettes? Why don't you give up?) — it can help researchers to access people's beliefs (whether rational or not).

Knowledge check 4

Give an example of a core study that was done in the 'field'.

Examiner tip

Although you do not manipulate the IV with a natural experiment, there is still an IV and a DV.

Knowledge check 5

What is the difference between a natural experiment and a field or laboratory experiment?

Examiner tip

You could be asked to design an experiment. Make sure you are clear about the differences between the three types of experiment.

Self-reports involve research that uses the participants' own account of their behaviour or experience. Self-report methods include questionnaires, interviews, thinking aloud and diary methods.

Knowledge check 6

Outline (a) two types of interview and (b) two types of questionnaire.

There are different kinds of questions that you could include in any self-report measure. Closed questions usually have a limited range of answers, while open questions allow a free response.

The following are examples of **closed** questions:
(1) Do you like dogs?
　　　Yes/No
(2) How much do you like studying psychology?
　　　Not at all　　1　　　2　　　3　　　4　　　5　　　a lot
(3) How much chocolate do you eat?

Two or more bars per day ☐
One bar per day ☐
4–6 bars per week ☐
1–3 bars per week ☐
1–4 bars per month ☐
Less than one bar per month ☐

(4) Which of the following aspects of your school do you like/enjoy? (You may tick more than one.)

The lessons ☐
The food ☐
The teachers ☐
Seeing your friends ☐
Sports activities ☐
Other activities ☐

(5) I like taking the lead in a group situation.

Agree ☐
Disagree ☐

The following are examples of **open** questions:
(1) What do you think about dogs?
(2) How much do you like studying psychology?
(3) How often do you eat chocolate?
(4) What aspects of your school do you like/enjoy?
(5) How do you behave in a group situation?

You can see that closed questions generally lend themselves to *quantitative data*, while open questions give *qualitative data*.

Finally, note that self-report techniques are sometimes used *as part of* an experimental method as a way of measuring the DV (see Experiment 5 on page 11).

Correlation

In a **correlation** usually, two 'measurements' are taken from the same set of participants. For example, we could get a sample of ten participants and for each of them measure their height (cm) and the length of their right foot (cm). The results are plotted in Figure 1.

Examiner tip
Before you choose open or closed questions, think about exactly what it is you want to find out. Also think about the type of data you want to gather. In other words, think through everything you are proposing before you start to write any answer.

Examiner tip
You may be asked to compare one method (such as the experimental method) with another (such as the self-report method).

Correlation is, in a way, a statistical technique rather than a method itself. It looks at whether two variables or factors are related.

Figure 1

The graph shows an overall upward movement. This is a **positive correlation**: as one variable increases (height), so does the other variable (length of foot).

What conclusions can we draw from such a correlation? Can we say that being tall *causes* people to have bigger feet? No. Can we conclude that having big feet *makes* you tall? No. All we can conclude is that the two variables are associated. We can *never* draw conclusions about cause and effect, however tempting this may be, when scattergraphs show a strong relationship between two variables.

There are essentially two types of correlation:
(1) Positive correlation: as one variable increases, the other variable increases.
(2) Negative correlation: as one variable increases, the other variable decreases.

Of course there might also be no correlation. When setting up research using a correlational design, you need to think about collecting two sets of data from each participant. Some examples are given below.

STUDY F, correlation between confidence and ability to write essays

A student researcher notices that some people in her class seem very confident about everything they say and do, but wonders whether this relates to how *good* they are at what they do. Also, some people seem quite low in confidence and uncertain, but as you get to know them you find out they have little ground for this — they are getting very good results. The student decides to investigate it. She draws up a table and approaches 12 people in her class. She asks each person to rate how confident they feel about their academic ability on a scale of 1 to 10. She then asks them to note down the last three scores for their essays and adds them up.

Figure 2

When she plots the scores on a scattergraph (Figure 2), she can see that there is an inverse relationship — a negative correlation — between the two variables. As confidence rating increases, the total score on the last three essays (academic performance) decreases.

What is the difference between a correlation and an experiment? This is a fundamental question. The difference is that, with an experiment, the IV is manipulated; but with a correlation, the two variables are just measured. Let us look at an example. You may have noticed that it can be hard to concentrate when it is too hot. Below are two studies, both concerned with temperature and concentration. In both studies, concentration is measured in the same way — by a computer task where participants listen to a radio programme through a computer. Each participant has been instructed to hit the space bar on the computer every time the radio presenter says a particular word. If the participant loses concentration, he or she will miss the word. The computer records how long (in seconds) the participant continues to concentrate without missing any target word.

Study 1. The researcher sets up two quiet rooms. One room is heated up to 35°C (equivalent to a very hot summer day in England). Another room is kept at a cool temperature of 15°C (equivalent to a typical October day in England — you would want to wear a coat if you were not moving around). Participants are allocated randomly to one of the two rooms and enter the room. After 10 minutes they start doing the concentration task.

Study 2. Participants are given the concentration task in a quiet room. The temperature is recorded while they are doing the task.

Which one is the experiment and which one is the correlation? You should have worked out that Study 1 is the experiment. The researcher manipulated one of the variables (which is therefore the IV for this study) by setting up the two conditions of the hot room and cool room. In contrast, in Study 2 the researchers did not control

> **Examiner tip**
>
> It is crucial that you know the difference between an experiment and a correlation. If you muddle up the two in an exam answer, you will score very low marks. An experiment has an IV and a DV; a correlation does not.

the temperature but simply measured it for each participant at the time of doing the concentration test. Therefore Study 2 cannot be an experiment and is, in fact, a correlational study.

Observation

In an observation, data are collected through observing or watching participants. In the earlier days of psychology, someone had to sit there and watch and take notes. This is not always necessary now as CCTV can be used. One-way mirrors are also commonly used so that participants do not feel too inhibited by seeing someone watch them.

Observational methods include:
(1) Controlled observation: this takes place in a controlled environment such as a laboratory. Participants might be given a particular task to do.
(2) Natural observation: this takes place in a natural environment (i.e. a situation which is natural for the behaviour the researcher is interested in).
(3) Participant observation: this is a special kind of natural observation. The observer (researcher) becomes a member of the community he or she is observing. For example, to investigate what teachers talk about in the staffroom and how their behaviour changes when they are not in front of students, the participant observer would have to become a teacher (or trainee teacher). With this method, the teachers should behave entirely naturally around the observer and may not even be aware that they are being observed.

For each of these observational methods, there are different ways of setting up the 'observation schedules'.
(1) Unstructured observation: the observer notes down or records all the behaviour with no predetermined ideas or categories.
(2) Structured observation: the observer has a predetermined schedule of observation. This could involve:
(a) event sampling — where the researcher is looking for certain behaviours and a tally chart or record is kept of every instance of these behaviours
(b) time sampling — where the researcher decides in advance to note down or record the behaviour present at certain times (e.g. at 1-minute intervals)

As with self-report, observation can be used as a technique within an experiment (or a correlation for that matter) for measuring one variable. For example, see Experiment 1, where the measure of 'shakiness' was by observing hand stillness/shakiness (and then rating it).

Case study

A case study is a detailed piece of research with a small number of participants (sometimes just one). There are various reasons why a case study might be favoured:
- The person or something about the person might be highly unusual, so that it would be very difficult or impossible to find a sample of 12 or more. Thigpen and Cleckley's study of multiple personality disorder in Eve is a good example of this. Other possible examples include someone suffering from a rare physical disease or someone who has undergone some unusual experience (e.g. operation or upbringing).

OCR A2 Psychology

- 'The case of Genie' involved a rare example of a child who had been horrifically abused and neglected as a child; the case study charts her subsequent attempts to live a 'normal' life.
- John Money's famous case study of David Reimer is another example. David was born a boy but, when his penis was accidentally burnt off in an operation as a baby, his parents were advised to bring him up as a girl — and David became Brenda. The case study and subsequent revisions to it (Diamond 1997) show an interesting (though ultimately tragic) interplay of environment and genes in determining a person's gender identity.

- The person might be considered to be highly illustrative of people with a particular condition or in a particular circumstance, even though the condition or circumstance may not be statistically rare (e.g. someone with schizophrenia, autism or dementia). Another possibility is a case study of a small number of 'normal' people and how they make decisions at a key point in life (e.g. a case study of ten sixth-formers and how they make their decision about what to do when they finish their A-levels).
- The researcher might choose a small-scale study in terms of number of people in order to capture rich detail and show some of the complexity in the participants' lives.
- The case study might be an early stage of a larger programme of research, to help the researchers plan a well-designed experimental project.

Strengths and weaknesses of different research methods

Laboratory experiments

Strengths	Weaknesses
• Manipulation of independent variable can indicate cause-and-effect relationships • Increased control and accurate measurement increases overall validity • Standardised procedures mean that replication is possible	• Artificial conditions may produce unnatural behaviour, which means that the research lacks ecological validity • Results may be biased by sampling, demand characteristics or experimenter bias • Total control over all variables is never possible • There may be ethical problems of deception etc. • Some people regard the process as dehumanising, with participants being treated like laboratory rats by having something *done to them*

Field experiments

Strengths	Weaknesses
• Greater ecological validity because surroundings are natural • Less likelihood of demand characteristics (if people are unaware of the research taking place)	• Difficulties in controlling the situation, therefore more possibility of influence from extraneous variables • Difficult to replicate • Can be time-consuming • Ethical problems of consent, deception, invasion of privacy etc.

Natural experiments

Strengths	Weaknesses
• Greater ecological validity, since the change in the independent variable is a natural one • Allow researchers to investigate variables that would be impractical to manipulate or investigate in other ways • Increased validity of findings due to lack of experimenter manipulation • If subjects are unaware of being studied there will be little bias from demand characteristics	• Difficult or impossible to infer cause and effect due to lack of control over extraneous variables and no manipulation of independent variable • Often difficult to replicate exactly • May be subject to bias if participants know they are being studied • Ethical problems of consent, deception, invasion of privacy etc., though it is often possible to overcome these

Self-reports

Strengths	Weaknesses
• Allow researchers to access a person's reasons for behaviour as well as otherwise unobservable psychological aspects such as attitudes and beliefs, past experiences, dreams etc. • Large amounts of data can be collected relatively quickly and cheaply, which can increase the representativeness and generalisability of the results • They are easy to replicate, especially in the case of a questionnaire • Closed questions are easy to score/analyse • Open questions can generate rich qualitative data	• People may not tell the truth — they may only tell us what they can remember (and memory is not perfect), or what they think we want to hear (demand characteristics and social desirability) • Questions or scales may be interpreted differently by different participants • Closed questions may force people into choosing answers that do not reflect their true opinions and therefore may lower the validity • Open questions are very difficult and time-consuming to score/analyse

Observations

Strengths	Weaknesses
• High ecological validity where 'real' behaviour is being observed — especially where people are unaware of being observed • Can produce extremely rich data if unstructured observation or participant observation is used • Low demand characteristics where people are unaware of being observed • Can be used where it would be difficult or unethical to manipulate variables • Can be used to generate hypotheses for further experimental research	• Lack of control over variables, as difficult to hold extraneous variables constant in a natural observation (though high control is possible in a 'controlled observation') • Difficult to conclude cause-and-effect relationships as no variables are being manipulated • Can be subject to observer bias • Can be difficult to ensure inter-rater reliability • Difficult to replicate natural observations as the circumstances may be unique (however, a good replication of controlled observation is possible) • Ethical issues if people are observed without their permission in a non-public area; also, issue of deception if the observer, in order to obtain data, pretends to be something he or she is not • Problems of demand characteristics if people are observed with their permission

Correlation

Strengths	Weaknesses
• Gives precise information on the degree of relationship between variables • No manipulation is required, so correlation can be used in situations where experimentation would be impossible or unethical • In some cases, strong significant correlations can suggest ideas for experimental studies to determine cause-and-effect relationships	• No cause and effect can be inferred • Technique is subject to any problems associated with the method used to collect data (e.g. self-report or observation may have been used to measure variables)

Case studies

Strengths	Weaknesses
• There are some circumstances where it is impossible to have a large number of participants, making case studies ideal • They usually generate a large amount of detail and rich qualitative data, which can give a very full picture of the situation under scrutiny	• Case studies rarely produce enough quantitative data for statistical testing; this means that some people regard case studies as little more than anecdotal evidence • Because case studies sometimes involve quite an intense relationship between the researcher and the participant, they may lack objectivity; the researcher may become too involved and may alter the natural course of the participant's life events and experiences

Knowledge check 8

Give one disadvantage of conducting a study in a laboratory.

Knowledge check 9

Give one advantage of conducting a field experiment.

Knowledge check 10

Using an example, give one advantage and one disadvantage of an observation.

After studying this section, you should know:
- the different methods required by the OCR specification
- the different types of each method
- the advantages and disadvantages of each method and type
- examples from core studies of each method and type

Summary

Operationalising variables

This is where the skill (and creativity) comes into psychology. You want to find out whether the independent variable (IV) affects the dependent variable (DV). But how do you measure the DV? You want a way of measuring the DV which is both **valid** and **reliable**.

Usually, there is more than one way to measure the DV; it might involve one of the following:
- getting the participants to do a task which measures the DV
- self-report, with participants answering a single question or a series of questions designed to measure the DV, administered as an interview or as a questionnaire
- psychometric tests (really a subtype of self-report)
- observation, with researchers watching the participants and counting the frequency of specific behaviours, or rating the participants for how intensely a specific behaviour is exhibited

Examiner tip

Students often confuse reliability with validity. Make sure than you don't make this mistake. Look at page 22 for definitions and examples.

- physiological measures — the use of blood tests, urine tests, blood-pressure tests, respiration rate tests etc. to measure DVs such as stress or excitement (i.e. processes which have notable physiological effects within the body)

Imagine you want to find out whether age affects memory. How can you measure memory? Here are some possibilities (with a few comments).

	Different ways of measuring memory	Comments
1	Give participants a list of 20 words, presented one at a time for 3 seconds each. Then give a distraction task such as some sums (this ensures the words will be recalled from long-term memory rather than short-term memory). Then ask participants to recall the words.	+ Objective and **reliable** + Gives a score – Not a very natural task (low **ecological validity**)
2	Show participants a short video clip and then ask (say) 10 questions about the film, such as: 'What colour was the woman's handbag?', 'What happened immediately after the woman left the room?' It could be a multiple-choice test.	+ Objective + Gives a score + A bit more natural than no. 1 above
3	Ask participants to keep notes/a mini-diary on a particular aspect of their life (e.g. food consumed at each meal time) for 7 days. This is then given to the researcher. The following week, ask a series of specific questions such as: 'Where did you go on Friday night?', 'What did you have for dinner on Thursday?', 'Which day did you meet your daughter for lunch?'	+ Asking about a person's own life has quite high ecological validity – It only tests one type of memory (autobiographical memory) – Each test would have to be individually tailored for each participant, leading to problems for reliability
4	Give participants a standard 'memory inventory' — a type of sophisticated questionnaire with a large number of questions or statements. One of these is called the Everyday Memory Questionnaire (Sunderland, Harris and Baddeley 1983) and asks about a whole range of possible memory failures, such as 'forgetting that you were told something yesterday or a few days ago, and having to be reminded about it' or 'finding that a word is on the tip of your tongue'. The participant has to rate each one on a scale of 1 to 9, where 1 represents 'not at all in the last 6 months' and 9 represents 'more than once a day'.	+ High reliability + Quite high validity in that each item refers to a real-life scenario – Validity may be lowered as people want to show themselves in a good light – Validity may be lowered if people's memory is quite bad, as they may forget that they forgot something

In another study researchers are interested in whether regular exercise makes people feel happier. Here are some possible ways of measuring happiness, with comments.

	Different ways of measuring happiness	Comments
1	Self-report: ask participants a single question, e.g. 'Are you generally happy? Yes or No?'	+ Quick, easy and cheap – Gives people only a very forced choice – Gives only **nominal data** (see section on 'Data', pages 32–41) – Social desirability: people might say what they think they *should* say, rather than what they really think

2	Self-report: ask participants a single question, e.g. 'On a scale of 1 to 10, how happy are you at the moment in your life?', where 1 = not at all happy and 10 = completely happy.	+ Quick and easy + Gives a score for each person (i.e. **ordinal** rather than **nominal** data) − Social desirability
3	Observation: get participants' everyday colleagues and family (i.e. people who see the participant on a daily basis) to rate the participants' behaviour on a happiness rating scale.	+ Captures a fuller picture of the participants' happiness, so likely to have good validity and high ecological validity − May be some problems of **reliability** (identified by inter-rater reliability) between observers
4	Physiological test: could test blood for level of endorphins (these are chemicals produced by the body which help give people a sense of wellbeing).	+ Objective − Does not account for participants' own subjective views of whether or not they feel happy

You sometimes also need to consider how to operationalise the IV. If the IV is sex, this is obvious — the two conditions will be male and female. However, sometimes you will have to operationalise more carefully. In the examples given above, the research questions were:

(a) Does age affect memory?

(b) Does regular exercise increase happiness?

The IVs are (a) age and (b) regular exercise. It is best for research projects at this level to include *two* conditions only (more than that makes the data analysis complicated).

Here are a couple of possibilities for each IV.

	Operationalisation of IV: age	Comments
1	Two groups: Group A is aged 30 years+, Group B is aged 18–25.	NB: You cannot manipulate age so, strictly speaking, this is a natural experiment. + Two groups and it is clear who would be in each group − Maybe the two groups are too close in age? − There could be a lot of variation in age in the first group
2	Two groups: Group A is aged 50–55, Group B is aged 20–25.	+ Clear distinction between both groups; a good age gap between them + Both groups are similarly defined
3	Three groups: Group A is aged 20–25, Group B is aged 40–45 and Group C is aged 60–65.	− Three groups is a nice idea, but at this stage it is unlikely the suggested statistical test will cope with more than two conditions

	Operationalisation of IV: regular exercise	Comments
1	Two groups. Group A is given a new programme of exercise involving attendance at a gym three times a week for 1 month. Prior to taking part in this study, they all report taking little or no exercise. Group B is given no new programme and they are selected because they report that they do little or no exercise (the control group).	NB: This would make the study a **true experiment** as the researcher is manipulating the IV. + The participants are similar before the experiment begins in terms of their normal amount of exercise + The two groups are clearly defined and distinct

2	Two groups. Group A reports that they take regular exercise (i.e. minimum of three times a week of 30 minutes' cardiovascular exercise). Group B reports that they do not take regular exercise (the control group).	NB: This makes the study a **natural experiment** because the conditions of the IV have occurred all on their own. + Has quite specific criteria (minimum of three times a week of 30 minutes' cardiovascular exercise) in order for a participant to be eligible for Group A − Deciding which group people are in depends heavily upon them telling the truth and remembering accurately how much exercise they do − There might be important differences between Groups A and B in other respects. For example, it is possible that Group A people are happier, more motivated, have more positive self-esteem etc., and that is why they exercise in the first place. This might affect the validity of the study as these 'other things' (extraneous variables), and not just the IV, might be influencing the DV.
3	Three groups, all of whom previously did no exercise. Group A has to do three cardiovascular exercise sessions a week. Group B has to do three sessions a week of cardiovascular *and* weight training exercise. Group C continues to do no exercise (the control group).	+ Good idea, all the groups are clearly defined etc., but − Having three groups makes the data analysis (statistical testing) very tricky and is best avoided

Looking at the comments above, you can see there are two important things to take into account when deciding how to operationalise the variables — namely, the validity and reliability of the measures.

There are many aspects of validity. These include:

- **Ecological validity:** does it reflect a naturally occurring task or behaviour (high ecological validity) or is it highly unusual (low ecological validity)?
- **Construct validity:** does the task measure a concept or construct which really exists?
- **Face validity:** does it appear to be a valid task?

If you applied a measure of reliability to the same person a couple of days later, you should get a similar result. When you are deciding how to operationalise a variable, you will also need to consider the *nature of the data* you will be able to collect. That will be further discussed in the section on 'Data' (pages 32–41).

Writing hypotheses

Once you have decided how to operationalise your variables, you can write your hypotheses.

The **research** (or '**alternate**') **hypothesis** is a statement of what you predict will happen — generally that there will be a difference in the DV between the two

Validity is concerned with whether an experiment or procedure for collecting data actually measures or tests what it claims to measure or test.

Reliability is the consistency of the measurement or *repeatability*.

conditions (for an experiment) or that there will be a correlation between the two variables (for a correlation). Research hypotheses can be **one**- or **two-tailed**:

- **One-tailed hypothesis:** this is when you predict the direction of the relationship between the two variables.
- **Two-tailed hypothesis:** this is when you think there will be a relationship between the variables, but you do not know the direction of the relationship.

The **null hypothesis** is a statement that there is no difference between the two conditions or that the IV has no effect on the DV (in the case of an experiment), or that there is no correlation between the two variables.

Here are some examples.

Research hypotheses (alternate hypotheses)		Null hypotheses
One-tailed	**Two-tailed**	
Males will score significantly higher on an extrovert inventory (as measured by the Eysenck Personality Inventory) than females.	There will be a significant difference between the male and female scores on a test of extroversion (as measured by the EPI).	There will be no significant difference between the male and female scores on a test of extroversion (as measured by the EPI).
Participants aged over 30 years will form significantly faster first impressions of a fictional stranger than younger participants aged between 18 and 25 years.	There will be a significant difference in the speed at which participants form first impressions of a fictional stranger, comparing participants aged over 30 years and those aged between 18 and 25 years.	There will be no significant difference in the speed at which participants form first impressions of a fictional stranger, comparing participants aged over 30 years and those aged between 18 and 25 years.
The witnesses of a staged crime will more frequently, at an identity parade, pick out someone who is wearing clothing similar to that worn by the culprit than pick out the real culprit when wearing different clothes.	There will be a significant difference in the number of times witnesses of a staged crime will, at an identity parade, pick out someone who is wearing clothing similar to that worn by the culprit compared to the number of times they will pick out the real culprit when wearing different clothes.	There will be no significant difference in the number of times witnesses of a staged crime will, at an identity parade, pick out someone who is wearing clothing similar to that worn by the culprit compared to the number of times they will pick out the real culprit when wearing different clothes.
People who own dogs will have lower stress scores than people who do not own dogs.	There will be a difference in stress scores between people who own dogs and people who do not own dogs.	There will be no difference in stress scores between people who own dogs and people who do not own dogs.
There will be a negative correlation between the number of absences from school and GCSE results.	There will be a correlation between the number of absences from school and GCSE results.	There will be no correlation between the number of absences from school and GCSE results.

In order to achieve full marks for writing hypotheses, the main thing is to ensure that you have enough detail in terms of the operationalisation of the variables. The following are examples of good and bad hypotheses:

Examiner tip

The hypothesis is always one-tailed or two-tailed. The null hypothesis is never one- or two-tailed because it states that there is no difference (or correlation).

Examiner tip

If your method is an experiment, it should be clear from your hypothesis what your IV and DV are. Look at the examples. Can you identify the IV and DV?

Knowledge check 11

Write a hypothesis for the 'sheep–goat' effect measured by the number of Zener cards correctly guessed out of 20. Make it two-tailed. ('Sheep' and 'goats' are believers and non-believers in ESP (extra-sensory perception).)

	Bad/dubious hypotheses	Good hypotheses
1	There will be a difference between males and females in terms of their memory (two-tailed).	There will be a significant difference between males and females on memory scores as recorded by the Everyday Memory Questionnaire (two-tailed).
2	People who exercise will be happier (one-tailed).	Participants who embark upon a three-times-weekly exercise programme will have higher levels of endorphins than participants who continue to take no exercise (one-tailed).
3	Older people will be less extroverted (one-tailed).	Participants in the age group 50–55 years will have significantly lower scores on the EPI than participants in the age group 20–25 years (one-tailed).

When you consider the difference between the bad/dubious hypotheses and the good ones, you should see why it is important to plan through the operationalisation of the variables *before* you write the hypotheses. The same level of detail should be given in the null hypothesis too.

Experimental designs

For any experimental method (field or laboratory), the researcher has to choose a design. Let's consider a new experiment.

An **experimental design** is how participants are allocated to the conditions of the independent variable.

STUDY G, Experiment 6

We want to find out whether time of day affects memory. Twelve participants are recruited and each is given a memory test separately.

- IV = time of day (morning at 10.30 a.m. or afternoon at 4.30 p.m.)
- DV = memory (score on memory test out of 20)

In order to measure the DV, the researcher gives each participant a list of 20 words, each projected on a screen for 3 seconds. After a 1-minute distraction task of some easy sums, they are asked to write down as many words as they can remember. Their score out of 20 is recorded.

There are three types of design:

(1) Independent measures design: each participant is in just one group — in this case either the morning group *or* the afternoon group.

(2) Repeated measures design: each of the participants will take part in *both* conditions — in this case, they will do the task in the morning *and* in the afternoon.

(3) Matched pairs design: you match the participants in each group for important participant variables which might extraneously affect the DV. In the case of Experiment 6, these would be sex and age, and possibly intelligence.

These are represented in Figure 3.

The following tables summarise the advantages and disadvantages of the different experimental designs.

Examiner tip
Make sure you are consistent in any examination answer. If you describe how participants are allocated to conditions, make sure you give each condition the correct label throughout your answer.

Independent measures design

Advantages	Disadvantages
• Each participant only experiences one condition so it might stop them guessing what the study is all about (and so reduce demand characteristics). • If participants drop out, you can just find someone else (see repeated measures and matched pairs disadvantages on page 26).	• You need twice as many participants for independent measures as you need for repeated measures. • This does not always adequately control for participant variables. The researcher may end up with participants in one group who are all somehow 'naturally' better at the DV than the participants in the other group, more intelligent, or more suited to the condition to which they have been allocated. This will skew the results.

Independent measures design	Repeated measures design	Matched pairs design
 A B	 A B	 A B
The 12 participants are each allocated to one condition, giving 6 in A and 6 in B. There are different participants in each condition.	The 12 participants take part in both conditions, A and B.	6 participants take part in condition A and 6 in condition B, but they are matched for important participant variables.

Figure 3

Repeated measures design

Advantages	Disadvantages
• This design controls for participant variables, because the participant variables in condition A are precisely the same as those for condition B! • Effectively, you can recruit half the number of participants you would for other designs. The example above shows that there will be 12 sets of data ($n = 12$) in each condition, while for the other designs there will only be 6.	• This design introduces another set of situational variables because doing one condition first may affect performance in the other condition. This can be due to either **fatigue effects** (the participants may become tired or bored the second time) or **practice effects** (participants may improve the second time because they know what to expect). This means that additional remedies might need to be built into the experiment, such as **counterbalancing** (some participants do A then B; the others do B then A). • Participants get to experience both conditions. This means they will have a better idea of the experiment and will be more prone to demand characteristics. • It may be that two different versions of the same task have to be prepared so that participants do not remember the 'answers' from the first time round. This means the researcher has to make sure that the tasks are of equivalent difficulty *and* they are themselves counterbalanced across the conditions. • If one participant drops out, you effectively lose two sets of data. • Some experiments would be impossible to do as a repeated measures design, e.g. if the conditions are A male and B female (someone cannot be both) or if the task has to be unique.

Matched pairs design

Advantages	Disadvantages
• Participant variables are controlled for because they are matched across the conditions. • There are no problems with **order effects**.	• If one participant drops out, you have to find another 'match' or risk losing two sets of data. • It can require hard work to match participants, especially on characteristics which need testing, such as IQ.

The matched pairs design perhaps avoids the worst disadvantages of the other two designs.

The choice of design will depend on exactly what the experiment involves. It is normally a toss-up between controlling for situational variables (order effects etc.) versus participant variables (a problem for an independent measures design). However, sometimes a repeated measures design is simply not possible — if the task can only be done once or if the IV is something which cannot be manipulated.

Control of extraneous variables

When experimental research is planned, it is important to anticipate all the factors that might affect the behaviour under scrutiny but which are not the focus of the research. You want to avoid these factors interfering with your research. The term

If we are conducting experimental research, we attempt to control as many variables as possible so that we can be sure that any changes in the dependent variable are due to the manipulation of the independent variable and not to any other variable.

for these factors is **extraneous variables**. Take an example where a researcher is interested in whether drinking coffee in the evening (IV) really does affect how well a person sleeps (DV). He has two groups of people — one group will drink coffee in the evening and another group will not. Then each person's sleep pattern will be monitored with an EEG and EOG (to monitor eye movements to track REM sleep) when they go to bed. Here is a list of factors that could affect how well the person sleeps *other than* the IV (drinking coffee in the evening or not):

(1) drinking coffee earlier in the day

(2) the *amount* of coffee drunk in the evening (e.g. 1 cup, 3 cups, 8 cups?)

(3) sleeping wearing an EEG head-net

(4) experiences in the evening (e.g. watching a particularly gripping film or doing yoga)

(5) ingesting other substances (e.g. cheese, chocolate, cannabis, red wine)

(6) the environment of the bedroom (e.g. noise and temperature levels)

(7) age of the participant

(8) sex of the participant

(9) how well the participant normally sleeps

(10) whether the experimenter is present at the time of going to sleep or not

(11) what the experimenter has said to the participant about the research

We do not want these extraneous variables to influence the DV because then we will not know whether the differences between the two groups' quality of sleep are caused by the IV or by the extraneous variables. The extraneous variables can be divided into several classes:

(a) situational variables (1, 2, 3, 4, 5, 6) — aspects of the research situation other than the IV which may influence the DV

(b) participant variables (7, 8, 9) — aspects of the participant's characteristics or experience (other than the IV) which may influence the DV

(c) experimenter variables (10, 11) — effects of the experimenter's (or 'investigator's') expectations which are somehow communicated (intentionally or unintentionally) to the participant (in a way, these are just another aspect of the situation, or a subtype of situational variable, but the specification mentions them specifically — so make sure you know them)

'**Demand characteristics**' are another type of extraneous variable. These are cues in an experimental situation which participants consciously or unconsciously pick up and which then cause them to alter their behaviour. In fact, just knowing that you are in a research situation may instantly make you subtly alter your behaviour so that you appear to be a 'good participant' or an 'interesting participant' or a participant who is going to help the researcher get the outcomes he or she is hoping for.

A researcher needs to anticipate as many extraneous variables as possible and put in as many controls as possible to avoid their influence. Much of this is just common sense, but there are also some standard 'tricks' and 'devices' that you should know for the exam, outlined in the following table.

Examiner tip

There are so many things which can be controlled that any examination answer could be just a long list of controls at the expense of equally important things. This is not desirable. Be selective. Perhaps control one (or two at most) situational, one participant and one experimenter variable.

Examiner tip

When you give an example of a control, explain what *type* of variable is being controlled.

Situational variables	Participant variables	Experimenter bias/ demand characteristics
• Keep the situation the same for everyone — use a laboratory or controlled environment so that temperature, noise and pleasantness of the environment are the same for everyone. • In a field study try to keep as many factors the same as possible (e.g. time of day). • **Procedural controls**: specifically instruct the participants to avoid doing certain things which might have an extraneous influence on the DV (e.g. ask them not to drink coffee at all during the day).	• Use a **matched pairs design**. • Use a **repeated measures design**. • Use an **independent measures design** but ensure that the participants are randomly allocated to each condition. In this way, any participant variables should be randomly/ equally distributed across conditions.	• **Single-blind technique**: participants are not told the aims of the study, so they cannot alter their behaviour in particular ways. • **Double-blind technique**: the researcher employs another researcher who only implements the procedure and does not know which condition the participant is in, or even what the aims of the research are. This means the researchers should not consciously or unconsciously influence the participants.

Sampling

The **target population** is the group to which research is hoping to generalise.

Your choice of participants is important. Key questions are:
• What group of people do you want to find out about? (This is the **target population**.)
• How much effort are you prepared to put in to make your sample **representative** of the target population?

Briefly consider the following scenarios. You are going to carry out a research project and all your participants will be people you know at sixth form.

Scenario 1: You want to conduct research to find out how open-minded sixth-formers are in your college. You are only interested in making conclusions about sixth-formers and so that is your target population — that is, the group to which you are aiming to generalise your research findings. Therefore, a sample of participants consisting only of sixth-formers will be suitable for your purposes (though there will still be some problems to consider — see page 29).

Scenario 2: You want to conduct research to find out how open-minded people in England are. Your target population is the population of England because you want to be able to generalise your findings to that group. Therefore, if your sample of participants consists only of sixth-formers, you will not be able to generalise to your target population.

Scenario 1: Sample of sixth-formers is representative of your intended target population — you can reasonably generalise your findings to the target population.

Scenario 2: Sample of sixth-formers is **not** representative of your intended target population — you cannot reasonably generalise your findings to the target population.

Figure 4

Scenario 1 is much better than scenario 2 for making generalisations and inferences about the target population. However, there still might be some problems. Can you make sure that your sample of sixth-formers is really like a little slice of the bigger cake, reflecting all the diversity within your sixth form? Ideally, you would want your sample to be as representative as possible in terms of aspects such as:

- gender balance
- ethnicity
- age range
- chosen subjects for A-level

Some sampling techniques will be more effective in achieving this than others. A number of different techniques are discussed in the next section.

Sampling techniques

Opportunity sample

The **opportunity sampling** technique involves the researcher approaching people who are easy to find and available. For example, you might approach people at your college whom you know, or who pass you in the corridor or happen to sit next to you in the library; or, if you are interested in the 'general public', you might approach people who walk past you in a shopping centre.

Advantages

- It is quick and easy to get participants. You can probably get quite a large sample quickly and without too much effort.

Disadvantages

- Participants are unlikely to be representative of the target population because you are more likely to encounter people like you (e.g. friends, people who do the same subjects or spend their free time in the same areas as you) and less

Examiner tip
Now you know about target populations and sample representativeness, think about how you would apply this to your study.

An **opportunity sample** is one that is selected by 'opportunity': the researcher simply uses the people that are present at the time that he or she is conducting the research.

likely to encounter people who are different from you. If, for example, you get an opportunity sample by approaching people in a shopping centre in order to research the 'general public', your sample is still going to be biased — people who go to shopping centres in the daytime might particularly like shopping, might not have a full-time job and so on.

Self-selecting sample (volunteer sample)

This involves the researcher advertising for participants. For example, if you want to look at the experiences of being a parent for adults who were themselves fostered as children, you will be unlikely to find participants through opportunity sampling. You would need to advertise for participants, for example in newspapers or on notice boards in GP surgeries. The people who reply are 'self-selecting' — that is, they have volunteered themselves for the research.

Advantages

- It is useful when the research requires participants of quite a specific type or with a specific experience.

Disadvantages

- Recruiting a sample can be expensive (advertisements in newspapers cost money, and the researcher may need to offer a fee) and it can take more effort.
- The type of people who volunteer to take part may be different in some ways from the type of people who are eligible but do not choose to volunteer. Perhaps they have more time, are more extroverted, or have a particular 'story' they want to tell. We can never really be sure that a self-selecting sample is representative of the target population.

Quota sample

This is rather like an opportunity sample; except that you identify certain subgroups within the target population, such as male/female or particular age groups, and fill up a quota of each so that your overall sample more closely matches the make-up of the target population.

Advantages

- It is more likely to be representative of the target population because of the representation of target groups.

Disadvantages

- Because you have still selected your sample opportunistically within the quota, there is likely to be some bias in how the people are selected.

Random sample

In a random sample, each participant is randomly selected from the target population. If the target population is students in your sixth form, you could achieve a random sample of 20 students by putting *every student's name* into a hat and picking out the first 20 names. There are also computer programs which can produce a random sample (e.g. there is a function in Excel). For a sample to be properly random,

A **random sample** is a sample that has been selected in a way that means everyone in the target population has an equal opportunity of being chosen.

each person in the target population must have an *equal probability of being selected*. (Contrast with systematic sample below.)

Advantages

- It is more likely to be representative than opportunity or self-selecting samples.

Disadvantages

- It can be time-consuming to get the right sample.
- Unless your target population is quite small, it is probably not easy to achieve a random sample.
- Some of the people picked by the random generator may not want to take part and will need 'replacing'; this may end up giving you, once again, some sort of biased sample.

Stratified sample

This is like a quota sample except that the quotas are selected through random sampling rather than opportunistic sampling.

Systematic sample

This is mentioned as a contrast to a random sample. In a systematic sample, every name from the target population is listed and then every *n*th person (e.g. every 20th person) is selected. This is *not* a random sample because not every person has an equal probability of being selected.

Number of participants

The final issue for sampling is: how many participants are needed? There is no fixed answer. Generally, the larger the sample, the better the chance that it will be representative of the population. However, when planning research there are practical considerations — getting a sample of 2,000 people may simply not be practical. So, what is sufficient? Most statistical tests work for samples of 10 for each condition, but having 20 or 40 would be much better.

Ethical issues

The British Psychological Society (BPS) has a code of conduct. The US equivalent is the code of the American Psychological Association (APA). The code of conduct helps researchers to avoid ethical problems in their research. The main guidelines are listed below. When planning your research project, remember to think through these guidelines and how they would relate to your intended research. You should try to make sure that it does not contravene any of the guidelines.

Protection of participants

Participants should not be harmed in any way (mentally or physically). Even when using self-report, asking participants about sensitive issues (e.g. difficult events in the past, problems with self-esteem) might cause distress and measures would have to be taken to avoid this.

Examiner tip
If you were conducting actual research, you would probably use an opportunity sample. If your study is hypothetical, you could easily describe how you would obtain a random sample.

Ethics are a set of rules designed to distinguish between right and wrong.

Informed consent

Participants should (in most cases) be asked if they want to take part in the study and they should be given all the relevant information about what it will involve, what the aims of the research are and so on. However, if the research is an observation in a public place (where people would normally expect to have their behaviour seen by other people) then consent is not necessary. For children, their parents or teachers should give consent; although consent is not required from the children themselves, it could be seen as 'good practice' to ask them too.

Right to withdraw

Participants should be told they can withdraw completely from the study at any time during and after the data collection. There should be no pressure to keep them in the study.

Deception

Participants should not be deceived about the aims of the study and should not be deliberately misled about any aspect of the study. For example, the use of a 'stooge' or 'confederate' would be considered to be deception by today's standards.

Anonymity and confidentiality

Participants' data and information about them should not be passed on to other people not directly involved in the research or published in a way which would reveal their identity.

Debrief

Participants, at the end of a study (except for a natural observation in a public place), should be told what was happening, asked if they had any concerns, and given any explanations they require. Anything which may have caused stress should be smoothed over so that the participant can leave the study in the same state in which he or she arrived.

Summary

After studying this section, you should know:
- how to write an appropriately one- or two-tailed hypothesis
- that the null hypothesis states no difference (or correlation) and thus is *not* tailed
- the different types of experimental design (repeated, independent and matched) and the advantages and disadvantages of each
- the importance of controlling extraneous variables (situational, participant and experimenter)
- about target populations and representativeness
- the different types of sample (such as random and opportunity) and know the advantages and disadvantages of different sample types

Data

When you are operationalising the DV, there are several further issues to consider. What sort of data will it produce (level of measurement)? What sort of table would you collect it in? Will you be able to display the data in a bar chart? Would the data fit the requirements of any inferential statistical test? This section will consider levels of measurement and some of the ways you can record and display the data.

Levels of measurement

There are four different kinds of scales or levels of measurement: nominal, ordinal, interval and ratio. These will be discussed in turn.

Nominal data

In nominal data, the number is just a label or name for a category (it does not have any genuine mathematical properties). Here are some everyday examples:

- Imagine a PE lesson at primary school where the teacher allocates each child to a team and calls each child '1' or '2'. Does this mean that the children in Team 2 are better than those in Team 1? Does it mean that Team 2 is twice as good as Team 1? No — it is just a 'label'.
- Think about Levi's jeans. There are Levi's 501s, 502s, 503s and so on, and even Levi's 765s. Does this mean that the 503s are better than the 501s? Are the 765s around half as good or half as big again as the 501s? No. The numbers are just names or (in this case literally) labels.

Some psychology research examples are shown on the following pages. The examples show you how to record and display nominal data. It is worth remembering that, for nominal data, you cannot use the measures of central tendency such as mean, median and mode. These are appropriate only for ordinal, interval and ratio data (and will be described in the next section).

STUDY H, Example I of study with nominal data, table of results and display of results

You want to find out whether male or female drivers are more likely to take a risk and return to their parked car *after* the pay-and-display ticket has expired. Having noted down times on the tickets displayed on the windscreens, you stand (discreetly) in view of a pay-and-display area. When someone returns to a car, you note down whether the person is male or female, and whether the car they drive away is within its time limit or not. The data collected look like this:

Male	Within time limit
Female	Within time limit
Male	Outside time limit
Female	Outside time limit

The data are then recorded in a two-by-two frequency table like this:

Two-by-two frequency table to show frequencies of males and females returning to car within and outside pay-and-display time limit

	In time limit	Outside time limit	Totals
Male	10	14	24
Female	19	3	22
Totals	29	17	

This could be displayed as a pair of pie charts or as a bar chart, as follows (Figures 5 and 6). Both of these clearly show that males are more likely than females to return to the car outside the time limit.

Figure 5

Figure 6

Remember, when you display data on charts, *always* label everything.

STUDY 1, Example 2 of study with nominal data, table of results and display of results

Participants are in one of three conditions: (A) a 1-month programme of cardiovascular exercise, (B) a 1-month programme of cardiovascular and weights exercise, or (C) no exercise. At the end of the month they are asked, 'Are you happy in general with your life?' Participants' responses are recorded individually and then compiled in a three-by-two frequency table:

Frequency table of number of participants reporting being happy versus not happy for each of the three conditions

	Happy: Yes	Happy: No	Totals
(A) Exercise: cardio	30	20	50
(B) Exercise: cardio + weights	31	19	50
(C) No exercise	16	34	50
Totals	77	73	150

NB This is the only example study with three conditions in this book. Generally, it is not a good idea to design a study for the exam with more than two conditions. However, if the data you collect are nominal, it is acceptable (because the inferential statistics test **chi-square** can handle it).

Data like these can also be displayed in a set of pie charts (Figure 7). They show clearly that a greater proportion of both the exercise groups reported feeling happy with their lives than the no-exercise group. It also appears that there was no real difference between the two exercise groups: whether the exercise is cardiovascular only or cardiovascular plus weights has little association with reported happiness.

Figure 7

It is also possible to use a bar chart, which again clearly shows how the proportion of the exercise groups who are happy is greater than that for the no-exercise group (Figure 8).

Figure 8 Bar chart showing the number of participants who said they were or were not happy in each of the three conditions

NB Don't forget that you cannot use mean, median or mode for nominal data. That is because there are no 'scores'. For example, you cannot work out the 'average' (mean) for Yes and No.

Again, remember to *label* axes etc. so that the information is presented clearly.

Ordinal data

Ordinal data involve numbers that can be put *in order* (hence the word *ord*inal) but do not have any other mathematical properties. As an everyday example, imagine Tom is asked to put six television programmes in order of preference where 6 is the most preferred and 1 is the least preferred.

6	Top Gear	Most preferred
5	Strictly Come Dancing	
4	Eastenders	
3	Holby City	
2	Mock the Week	
1	Supernanny	Least preferred

Top Gear is at the top. It has a score of 6. It is better in Tom's view than *Strictly Come Dancing* and *Eastenders* and so on, and it is certainly better than *Holby City*, which only got 3. However, does this mean that, according to Tom, *Top Gear* is exactly twice as good as *Holby City*? No. Does it mean that the difference in his liking between *Supernanny* and *Mock the Week* is exactly the same as the difference between *Eastenders* and *Strictly Come Dancing*? No. So the numbers can help put them in order, but there are no other mathematical properties. The distance between 6 and 5 is not necessarily equivalent to the distance between 3 and 4.

In psychology studies, most of the scores obtained from self-report questionnaires and rating scales are ordinal, as in the following examples:
- A rating scale asks you to rate how good your teacher is on a scale of 1 to 10.
- A short questionnaire consists of 20 questions on beliefs about yourself. Each question is presented as a statement to which the participant has to say 'Agree' or 'Disagree': for example, 'I usually think that I am at least as able as most of the people in the room — Agree or Disagree'. Each 'agree' statement is worth 1 point and they are all added together to produce a final score out of 20.
- Observers want to look at aggression levels in nursery school children. Each child's behaviour is noted, a behaviour coding scheme is applied to give each behaviour a score, and the scores are then added up.

For ordinal data, you can use **measures of central tendency** in order to summarise and display the data. There are several different kinds:
- The **mean** is 'the average'. Add up all the scores and then divide by the number of scores.
- The **median** is 'the middle value'. Put all the scores in increasing order. For a series of n scores, the middle score, the median, will be $(n + 1)/2$. For example:
  - When there are 11 scores, the middle value will be $(11 + 1)/2$ which equals 6. So the median is the value of the 6th score.
  - When there is an even number of values, let's say $n = 10$, then the middle value is $(10 + 1)/2 = 5.5$. So you have to find the 5th *and* the 6th and take the average (the mean) of the two.
- The **mode** is 'the most fashionable value'. Group all the scores of each value together. The value that has the most scores is the mode. Sometimes, there are two or more modes (especially in a small data set) — you should report them all.

Knowledge check 13

Give an example of ordinal data that will be evident in all athletics events at say the Olympic Games.

There are worked examples of mean, median and mode in Studies J and K below.

With ordinal data, you can also use **measures of dispersion**. These give you some idea of how 'spread out' your data are. There are a number of measures of dispersion (e.g. standard deviation, inter-quartile range), but the most important one to know is the **range**. This is simply, for any set of data, the difference between the top value and the bottom value. This is also given in the studies below.

Study J is an example of a study involving ordinal data.

STUDY J, example of study containing ordinal data

A researcher wants to find out whether women who have recently had a baby have any signs of memory problems. The researcher finds 10 women who have given birth in the last 3 months, and 10 women who are not mothers (the control group). Each person in the control group is matched to someone in the birth group on the basis of age and IQ score. Each of the 20 women is given the Everyday Memory Questionnaire, which asks about 27 possible memory failures, such as 'When talking to someone, forgetting what you have just said. Maybe saying, "What was I talking about?"' or 'Doing something routine twice by mistake, e.g. putting two lots of tea in the teapot'. The participant has to rate each one on a scale of 1 to 9, where 1 represents 'not at all in the last 6 months' and 9 represents 'more than once a day'. The higher the score, the greater the memory problems.

Data are collected in the following table:

Participant number	Recent mothers' scores	Control group scores
1	49	58
2	57	56
3	44	34
4	59	29
5	49	69
6	24	60
7	60	47
8	52	66
9	59	71
10	38	60
Total	491	550

Calculations for mean, median, mode and range

Mothers' group	Control group
Mean = 491/10 = 49.1 Mothers' group's scores arranged in ascending order: 24, 38, 44, 49, 49, 52, 57, 59, 59, 60 Median is middle value (halfway between 5th and 6th): 50.5 Mode = 49 and 59 Range = 60 − 24 = 36	Mean = 550/10 = 55 Control group's scores arranged in ascending order: 29, 34, 47, 56, 58, 60, 60, 66, 69, 71 Median is middle value (halfway between 5th and 6th): 59 Mode = 60 Range = 71 − 29 = 42

This can be summarised in a table of measures of central tendency and dispersion. The bar chart gives a visual display of the means, neatly summarising the results (Figure 9).

	Recent mothers' scores	Control group's scores
Mean	49.1	55
Median	50.5	59
Mode	49, 59	60
Range	36	42

Figure 9 Bar chart comparing mean scores on Everyday Memory Questionnaire for new mothers and control group

Interval level data and ratio level data

Interval level data are 'one step better' than ordinal data. While with ordinal data we could say that a rating of 6 was more than a rating of 5, we could not be sure that the difference between 5 and 6 meant the same as the difference between 7 and 8. However, with interval level data, the points are evenly spaced. The intervals between them are equal (hence 'interval level data'). To take an everyday example, the difference between 35°C and 40°C is the same as the difference between 20°C and 25°C.

Ratio level data are the highest, most precise level of measurement. Unlike interval level data, their 0 really does mean 0. Often the two kinds of data are grouped together and referred to as 'at least interval level data'. The following are some examples from psychology which are 'at least interval level data':

- the score from an IQ test or other psychometric test
- in an observation of a person's body language, a count of how many times someone touches their ears when in conversation with someone else
- the time taken to complete a cognitive task
- the number of words remembered on a test of memory
- the number of micrograms of adrenaline in a urine test (as a test for stress)

An example of a study with 'at least interval level data' follows. You will see that the summary and descriptive data really do differ from those for ordinal data. (There is also a difference in the inferential statistical tests you can use, see pages 41–44).

Knowledge check 14

Why are interval data often said to be 'one step better' than ordinal data?

STUDY K, example of study with interval/ratio level data

A researcher wants to find out if people who start playing a musical instrument increase in intelligence (as measured by an IQ test). Ten children (aged between 8 and 10) who take up a musical instrument are given an IQ test before their first lesson. Two months later they are given another version of the IQ test.

The results are recorded in a table as follows:

	IQ before music lessons	IQ after music lessons
1	99	101
2	104	103
3	140	148
4	135	138
5	126	124
6	100	97
7	98	110
8	107	107
9	110	109
10	120	121
Totals	1139	1158

Because the same participants take part in both conditions — before music lessons and 2 months after music lessons — this is a **repeated measures design**.

Calculations for mean, median, mode and range

Before music lessons	After music lessons
Mean = 1139/10 = 113.9 Scores arranged in ascending order 98, 99, 100, 104, 107, 110, 120, 126, 135, 140 Median value (5.5th value) = 108.5 No mode Range = 140 – 98 = 42	Mean = 1158/10 = 115.8 Scores arranged in ascending order 97, 101, 103, 107, 109, 110, 121, 124, 138, 148 Median value (5.5th value) = 109.5 No mode Range = 148 – 97 = 51

**Table of summary of results: measures of central tendency
for children before and after taking music lessons**

	IQ before music lessons	IQ after music lessons
Mean	113.9	115.8
Median	108.5	109.5
Mode	No mode	No mode
Range	42	51

Figure 10 Bar chart showing mean IQ scores for children before taking music lessons and after

The mean for each group can be displayed on a bar chart (Figure 10). While we can see in the raw data table that most of the participants' IQ scores improved after music lessons, a comparison of the means indicates that it is not a very big difference overall.

Advice on displaying data

Remember, the purpose of displaying data is to *show* people clearly what the outcomes are. Each table or graph should contain all the information so it can stand alone — that is, it should tell the whole story without depending on the text. Below are some 'dos and don'ts' for displaying data.

Dos

✔ Give tables and graphs a *title*.
✔ On a bar chart label the y-axis (vertical axis). We need to know what the numbers indicate: number of participants? mean scores? percentage? number of bars of chocolate? Without a label, the reader will not know — and the examiner will not give you a mark.
✔ On a bar chart, make sure you label what or who the bars represent — that is, the condition each represents. You can do this by labelling the *x*-axis (horizontal axis).
✔ On a pie chart, each slice of pie should be labelled clearly to show which group the slice represents. Putting in the percentage is also a good idea.

Don'ts

✘ Do not use a long table of each participant's scores in order to summarise data. While you would *record* your data (your *raw* data) as you go along, participant by participant, this is not a *summary* of the data. To summarise data you need to use either:
    ✔ for ordinal, interval or ratio data — measures of central tendency such as mean, median and mode
    ✔ for nominal data — a frequency table (e.g. two-by-two; see examples above)

✘ Do not draw bar charts of data for each participant (see Figure 11).

OCR A2 Psychology

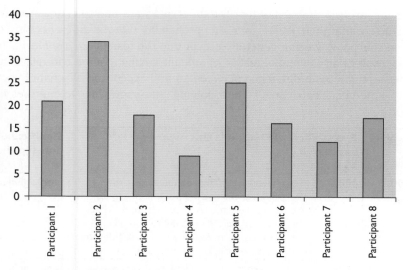

Figure 11 Don't draw a chart like this one — it does not give an overall summary of results!

After studying this section, you should know:
- what type of visual display to sketch for a particular set of data
- that full labels on every visual display are essential
- the different levels of measurement and how to identify each from a particular set of data
- how to calculate measures of central tendency and dispersion (mean, median, mode and range)

Summary

Inferential tests

What is the point of **inferential tests**? Suppose you find that you have got a difference between the two groups or the two conditions overall. For example, in Study J above, about the difference in memory scores between recent mothers and non-mothers, we could see that the mean memory score for the recent mothers was 49.1, while the non-mothers' mean memory score was 55. This is a difference of 5.9 points. Is this enough of a difference to be able to *conclude* that recent mothers' scores were genuinely and significantly worse? Is this enough of a difference to reject the null hypothesis and accept the experimental (or 'alternate') hypothesis? Or could this result have occurred simply due to chance factors? An inferential test helps to decide, by working out the *probability* of the *difference* between the two sets of scores occurring just due to chance (rather than because of any real effect). This probability (p) is expressed as a number between 0.00 and 1.00.

An **inferential test** helps to decide, by working out the *probability* of the *difference* between the two sets of scores, whether a result is due to chance rather than a real effect.

Significance

At what point does the probability of the differences having occurred due to chance factors mean that we can be sufficiently satisfied that the results are due to a genuine difference between the two conditions (i.e. that the IV really has had an effect on the DV)? The standard level for a test showing **significance** is $p \leq 0.05$. This means that

A result is said to be statistically **significant** if it is unlikely to have occurred by chance.

there is 5% (or less) probability that the differences are due to chance factors and so, conversely, that there is 95% (or more) probability that the differences are due to the IV. At this point, we can generally accept that the results are *significant*. To find that the result of an inferential test is significant means that we can reject the null hypothesis ('there is no difference between...') and accept the alternate hypothesis ('there is a difference between...'). The following table shows how to interpret various values of p.

Probability	Probability expressed as % chance	What does this mean?	Significant or non-significant?
$p = 1.00$	100%	There is 100% probability that the differences in the two sets of scores occurred due to chance factors. That is, there is 0% probability that the results occurred due to a real difference between the two conditions.	Non-significant
$p = 0.50$	50%	There is 50% probability that the differences between the two sets of scores occurred due to chance factors alone. That is, there is 50% probability that the results occurred due to a real difference between the two conditions.	Non-significant
$p = 0.10$	10%	There is 10% probability that the differences between the two sets of scores occurred due to chance factors alone. That is, there is 90% probability that the results occurred due to a real difference between the two conditions.	Non-significant
$p = 0.05$	5%	There is 5% probability that the differences between the two sets of scores occurred due to chance factors alone. That is, there is 95% probability that the results occurred due to a real difference between the two conditions.	Significant
$p < 0.05$	<5%	There is *less than* 5% probability that differences between the two sets of scores occurred due to chance factors alone. That is, there is more than 95% probability that the results occurred due to a real difference between the two conditions.	Significant
$p = 0.01$	1%	There is 1% probability that the differences between the two sets of scores occurred due to chance factors alone. That is, there is 99% probability that the results occurred due to a real difference between the two conditions.	Significant

For a correlation, an inferential test will tell us the probability that two variables are correlated (either positively or negatively). In the same way as above, if $p \leq 0.05$, we can reject the null hypothesis ('there is no correlation between...') and accept the alternate hypothesis ('there is a correlation between...').

Knowledge check 15

What is meant by $p < 0.05$ in psychology?

Knowledge check 16

If $p < 0.05$ in psychology, what does this mean in relation to the hypothesis?

There are some occasions where a researcher might want to set a more stringent level of significance and where a 5% probability of results occurring due to chance factors is in fact too high. Consider a non-psychological example: if a group of researchers is testing whether or not a particular drug reduces a cancerous tumour, they would probably want to be *more certain* that the drug really does work before their company starts to invest millions of pounds in producing this drug and convincing the NHS and others that it is worth prescribing. So they might set a level of $p \leq 0.01$ (i.e. only 1% probability it is due to chance factors and 99% certainty it is due to the drug).

Perhaps the drug has known side-effects which can be severe. In this case, the researchers would want even more certainty that the drug works. In this situation, they might only be satisfied with $p \leq 0.001$ (i.e. only 0.1% probability of differences occurring due to chance factors and 99.9% certainty they are due to the drug).

Type 1 and type 2 errors

As discussed above, we can (in normal circumstances) accept the alternate hypothesis when there is 5% probability that results occurred due to chance factors (and therefore 95% probability that the results occurred due to real differences between the two conditions). However, we are dealing only with probabilities and not absolute certainties. This means we can never be *absolutely sure* that our results mean what we think they mean. Even with a 5% probability that the results for two conditions occurred due to chance factors, we are *only* 95% certain. This means that sometimes we might accept the alternate hypothesis when actually the null hypothesis was true — a false positive. Conversely, there may be times when we reject the alternate hypothesis and accept the null hypothesis when actually the alternate hypothesis was true — a false negative. These are called type 1 and type 2 errors respectively:

Type 1 error	False positive	Accept alternate hypothesis although really the null hypothesis was true
Type 2 error	False negative	Accept the null hypothesis although really the alternate hypothesis was true

Obviously, which level of significance you apply affects your chances of making a type 1 or type 2 error. Researcher A, who sets a 'loose' level of $p \leq 0.05$, is more prone to make a type 1 error than researcher B, who sets a 'stringent' level of $p \leq 0.01$. However, researcher B is more likely to make a type 2 error and reject the alternate hypothesis even though it is true. There is always a chance you will make a mistake in one way or another (type 1 versus type 2) and accept the wrong hypothesis — that is the nature of probability.

Types of inferential test

You do not need to know *how* to do these statistical tests for examination purposes. However, you will be asked which test to carry out and why.

There are five different statistical tests you need to know about (though many others exist). These five are all **non-parametric tests**. Non-parametric tests are for use on data which are either (a) not 'normally distributed' (i.e. when you plot a frequency table or scores it is not in a bell shape) or (b) not of 'at least interval level' status (i.e. it is either nominal or ordinal). The following table sets out the five tests and explains when they should be used.

Test	When to use	Example study above where this test would be appropriate
Chi-square test	This is for **nominal data**, when data are in **categories** (e.g. tally charts). There are three types of chi-square test. A two-by-two (as in Study H), a three-by-two (as in Study I; this can be any number-by-any number) and a much less used 'one-sample' (e.g. absenteeism with categories of the five days of the week).	STUDY H and STUDY I
Sign test	This is used when you are looking for a **difference** between two conditions. It is for **ordinal data** for **repeated measures**. It is not a very powerful test, so generally to be avoided.	—
Wilcoxon signed ranks test	This is used when you are looking for a **difference** between two conditions. It is for **ordinal data** (or interval data if necessary) for a **repeated measures** design.	STUDY K
Mann–Whitney U test	This is used when you are looking for a **difference** between two conditions. It is for **ordinal data** (or interval data if necessary) for an **independent measures** design.	STUDY J
Spearman's rho rank correlation coefficient	This is a test of **correlation**. It is for **ordinal data** (though it can be used with interval level data if necessary). Remember, a correlation involves measuring two different variables for each of the participants.	STUDY F

Examiner tip

You will never need to calculate a statistical test. However, you do need to know what test is appropriate for the data you propose and why that test is appropriate.

Knowledge check 18

What test would you apply to data that are two-sample, ordinal, for a repeated measures design and if you are looking for a difference?

Knowledge check 19

Give four reasons why you would apply a Mann–Whitney test.

The specification does not require you to know about any parametric tests. However, in the exam you may design a study which involves interval level data (e.g. you are timing participants in seconds or they are taking an IQ test). In this situation, when asked which statistical test you would use, choose one of the non-parametric tests above which is for at least *ordinal* data and which suits your study, depending on whether you are looking for difference or correlation, and on the design.

Finally, note that, with the exception of the chi-square test, all the tests can cope with only *two* conditions or *two* groups. Therefore, remember that you should *not* design a study with many different conditions.

Summary

After studying this section, you should:
- be able to define and explain an inferential statistical
- be able to define and explain statistical significance
- know about levels of significance and when to accept or reject a hypothesis
- be aware of (and so avoid) type 1 and type 2 errors
- know the five types of inferential test
- know when to use each type of test

Approaches, perspectives, debates and issues in psychology

Approaches in psychology

An approach is a particular view as to why and how we think, feel and behave as we do. It is an area of research characterised by a particular focus or by a particular set of themes, outlooks or types of explanation. (Some psychologists would instead refer to the approaches named in the specification as *domains*.) The five approaches to be discussed below are the cognitive, physiological, individual differences, developmental and social approaches. For each approach a description will be given, and a strength and a weakness noted, followed by two or more examples from AS core studies or A2 options. It is also important for you to think of your own examples.

The cognitive approach

This approach concerns the mind and mental processes — how we think (rationally and irrationally), solve problems, perceive, make sense of and understand the world; how we use and make sense of language; how and why we remember and forget. The main assumption of the cognitive approach is that how we think is central in explaining how we behave and how we respond to different people and different situations.

In some ways, the cognitive approach sees a human as rather like a complicated computer — information enters the mind (input), it is processed and stored, and it is sometimes used again later (output) through remembering or responding to a situation.

A strength and weakness of the cognitive approach

- This is the part of psychology which genuinely engages in how we think. Many people regard this topic area as central to psychology.
- You cannot directly see how the mind works and so some critics of the cognitive approach think that it is not a valid area of study as it is really just guesswork.

Examples of the cognitive approach

(1) A core study example is the Loftus and Palmer study on memory. It shows how memory is not necessarily a perfect record of an event, but can be influenced by information after the event. Participants who were asked 'How fast was the car going when it smashed...?' were twice as likely to believe they had seen broken glass (when there was none) than those who were not asked the question. This study highlights the complex processes by which humans store and combine sensory inputs.

Cognitive psychology is about mental processes such as remembering, perceiving, understanding and producing language, solving problems, thinking and reasoning.

Knowledge check 20

Give a strength of the cognitive approach using an example.

Examiner tip

You should know at least two examples from psychological research of each approach.

Physiological psychology explores human behaviour and experience by looking at people as if they were biological machines.

Knowledge check 21

Give a weakness of the physiological approach using an example from AS and an example from A2.

Examiner tip

Don't just describe an example. Make sure you can say *why* it is an example of a particular approach.

Individual differences acknowledge that not all people are the same and that there are differences in life experience, intelligence etc.

(2) An example of a cognitive model from an A2 option is the Health Belief Model. It describes how different beliefs affect the likelihood of a person adopting any particular health behaviour. A person's overall decision is based on his or her beliefs and cognitions about a particular disease in terms of its likelihood of afflicting him or her, the severity of such an illness and so on. If you want to encourage people to adopt more healthful behaviours, you have to change their cognitions about the disease.

The physiological approach

This approach concerns the physiological or biological aspects of humans and how they affect our behaviour, thought patterns and emotional responses. In a way, this approach sees humans as complicated machines, with biological processes, such as hormone release and brain activity, governing our behaviour. Equally, the body and brain are altered by our experience of the world. Therefore, while much physiological research looks at how the body determines behaviour, there is also research which looks at how our experience shapes our brain development and so on.

A strength and weakness of the physiological approach

- This is the most scientific part of psychology, which genuinely uses the scientific method and scientific approaches to measurement of DVs.
- Often, physiological research shows only an association between a psychological event and a biological event as we do not know the direction of cause (i.e. which event caused the other). For example, in the case of Dement and Kleitman, we do not know whether dreaming *caused* the changes in EEG patterns, or if the changes in the brain waves caused the dreaming — or if something else (e.g. activity in a specific part of the brain) caused both things to happen together. A fair amount of physiological research faces this type of problem.

Examples of the physiological approach

(1) The core study by Dement and Kleitman shows how the physiology of the brain, in terms of patterns of brain waves, is linked to the psychological experience of sleep. In particular, the periods of rapid eye movement (REM) — characterised also by a fast, active brain pattern and very low muscle tension — are associated with a person's experience of dreaming. In fact, the pattern of the eye movements often matched the reported content of a person's dream.

(2) The A2 option study by Raine, Buschbaum and LaCasse shows, using PET scans of the brain, that there are differences in the brain activity between murderers (pleading Not Guilty by Reason of Insanity — NGRI) and non-murderers. The differences include less activity in the frontal lobe and the amygdala.

(3) The A2 option study by Martens (1990) distinguishes between somatic anxiety, which involves the physiological changes associated with high arousal, and cognitive anxiety, which involves the anxious thoughts that accompany somatic anxiety. Both physiological and cognitive factors interact in competition anxiety.

The individual differences approach

This approach is concerned with the differences between people (rather than the things we might have in common), particularly in terms of personality and abnormality. One of the assumptions of this approach is that there are differences between the people of any group, in terms of their personal qualities, the ways in which they respond to situations, their behaviour and so on, and that it is examining these differences that is the most revealing. Some research within the approach has focused on trying to measure these differences, for example through the use of psychometric tests such as IQ tests or personality tests. Some research has tried to categorise and identify different types of abnormality.

A strength and weakness of the individual differences approach

- This approach underlines the differences between us, and, arguably, takes a more *idiographic approach* to psychology (i.e. focuses on what makes each of us unique) rather than a *nomothetic approach* (i.e. one which focuses on the common features shared by human beings).
- There is a danger that, when investigating differences, *values* can come in. Which 'version' of human is better? Which personality is better? What is normality? Is abnormality (always) bad? Is more intelligence better than less intelligence? This can lead into murky and dangerous areas such as human *eugenics* — the idea of selective breeding in humans so that some traits are bred out. This was a fundamental idea of the Nazis and led to atrocities against humans, including ethnic minorities and homosexuals. (The Nazis believed and propagated an erroneous view that some ethnic minorities were less intelligent, had poor moral reasoning and so on. Some of this was based on methodologically unsound research.)

Examples of the individual differences approach

(1) The core study by Thigpen and Cleckley aimed to describe a specific disorder — multiple personality disorder (MPD; sometimes also called dissociative identity disorder). In a case study, the article outlines Eve's different personalities, how they each revealed themselves to the therapists, and the more objective tests (e.g. IQ tests, memory tests, EEG) that were undertaken in order to investigate whether or not Eve did in fact have multiple, separate personalities.

(2) The A2 option study by Daly and Wilson (2001) looked at differences between males and females in crime rates and proposed that the reason why males are more likely to commit crimes is their evolutionary histories — as hunter-gatherers, they would have been more likely to engage in risk-taking behaviour (and the risk-takers were perhaps more likely to survive and procreate as they would have been more 'successful' overall).

The developmental approach

This approach is concerned with how we change as we age and mature — in particular, how we change cognitively and socially. Much of the research has focused on the changes within childhood, as this is the fastest period of change in a person's life. Increasingly, however, over the last two decades, psychology has recognised the life-span approach and acknowledged the changes (social and cognitive) that continue to take place throughout all stages of adulthood. One key assumption of this approach is that events that happen to us early in life can have a long-term effect on the course

Examiner tip

Your examples to illustrate approaches could all come from the AS course because there are three examples of each approach on the specification. But that is boring! Show how brilliant you are and instead give an example from one or more of your A2 chosen options.

Knowledge check 22

Give an assumption of the individual differences approach.

Developmental psychology is concerned with change and development over time.

of our development. Another assumption is that people of the same age share much in common, in terms of cognitive abilities, issues they face and so on.

A strength and weakness of the developmental approach

- This approach emphasises growth and change and how an experience at one point in life can have various consequences at later stages. It helps us understand how people's life trajectories can be altered for better or worse, and therefore can make useful contributions to governmental policy in areas such as education, social work and housing policy.
- The developmental approach can imply that we are all carrying around huge amounts of baggage, that we are not really free to be whoever we want to be or do whatever we want to do, but rather have been formed by our early childhood experiences. Thus, the approach can be perhaps too **deterministic**.

Examples of the developmental approach

(1) The Samuel and Bryant core study looked at conservation, a key cognitive 'marker' showing whether a child has progressed from Piaget's 'pre-operational' stage to the 'operational' stage of thought (i.e. a more logical stage). This study focused on *cognitive* development. In particular, it investigated how aspects of the procedure (asking the key question once or twice) can affect children's ability to show that they can conserve. This study still supported a broadly Piagetian and developmental approach because it found that, in general, older children were less likely to make mistakes on conservation tasks of all types.

(2) An A2 option example is Erikson's psychosocial theory of development, a broadly psychodynamic model of the stages we go through as we get older. Unlike Freud, it concentrates more on the *social* aspects of development (who our 'significant others' are in any stage) as well as the psychological challenges and conflicts which are faced in any stage. For Erikson, for example, in the first stage of life (age 0–1) the main conflict is whether to trust or not trust, and the outcome depends on our interactions with our main carers (probably parents). The resolution of this conflict will impact on later life. One stage of particular interest to educational psychologists is stage 4, 'industry versus inferiority', because childhood experiences at school with peers and teachers (e.g. the degree of success in completing tasks, the extent of encouragement and acknowledgement received from others) will affect whether a person feels inferior or industrious towards educational (and broader) achievement. Erikson's is a broad-span, life-developmental approach.

The social approach

Areas of particular interest for social psychologists include interpersonal attraction and relationships, prejudice and discrimination, and group dynamics (including conformity, obedience and minority influence). It focuses in particular on how the individual behaves within these social situations. When we are looking for an explanation of why someone behaved the way he or she did, should we look at him or her as an isolated individual, or should we look at the individual in the context of the people around him or her? The social approach would say the latter — we can only understand people in the context of their interactions with and perceptions of others.

Knowledge check 23

Give a strength of the developmental approach using an example.

Examiner tip

Knowing examples of an approach is one thing, but can you go beyond this and give an example to illustrate the strength (and/or weakness) of an approach?

Social psychology is concerned with how humans interact with each other.

A strength and weakness of the social approach

- This approach contextualises the individual human in the social world. This is important because, fundamentally, we are social animals for whom status, relationships, intimacy and family really do matter. Psychology would not be complete without research into our social psychology.
- This is a very complex area to research and understand. Studying a human as a discrete entity is complex enough; studying humans in interaction increases the complexity exponentially. This means the research is complicated to design (especially in ways which are both ecologically valid and ethical), as well as to analyse and make valid inferences or conclusions from.

Knowledge check 24

Give an assumption of the social approach.

Examples of the social approach

(1) The Piliavin et al. core study belongs in the social approach because it shows how an individual's decision whether or not to help is a function of the social situation and his or her perception of that situation. The researchers found that the ill 'victim' (cane condition) was helped more frequently and more rapidly than the drunk 'victim' in the study on the subway. Men were more likely to help than women. If the emergency continued and the victim was not helped, people were more likely to say something to the observer or leave the immediate area of the emergency (the 'critical area'). Piliavin et al. explained these findings in terms of a 'model of response to an emergency situation'. This model makes the interesting claim that our decision to help or not is a function of wanting to reduce the anxiety ('psychological arousal') produced by witnessing an emergency. Various factors have an effect on the level of arousal. The higher the arousal, the more a bystander is motivated to do something in order to relieve this anxiety: one option is to help, though other options include walking away from the emergency scene. The following social factors are mentioned in the model:

(a) Physical proximity to the emergency — the closer the bystander, the higher the arousal and therefore the greater the need to take some action (helping or leaving) in order to reduce the arousal.

(b) Empathy with the victim — if the bystander can identify with the victim (e.g. is similar in age, sex or ethnicity) or believes the illness is not self-inflicted, the psychological arousal is greater and so there is increased likelihood of taking some action to reduce the arousal.

(c) If other people around are not helping, this may allow the individual to believe that it is not really an emergency (even though it is). This is sometimes called bystander apathy or pluralistic ignorance.

(d) The perceived costs versus rewards of helping or not helping — the individual makes a decision whether or not to help based on perception of costs of helping (e.g. likelihood of danger of being attacked, time spent) weighed against rewards of helping (e.g. reducing the arousal, feeling good about oneself, praise from the victim or other bystanders).

This study therefore illustrates how an individual does not make an isolated decision to help; rather, his or her individual perceptions of the social situation, the person who needs help and so on all have an effect on helping. Thus, helping is not (just) a function of an individual's personality (kind or altruistic), but a function of the social situation.

(2) An A2 option example concerns sport performance. Social facilitation occurs when a sport performance improves in the presence of an audience and social inhibition when a sport performance declines. Why is this? Zajonc (1965) suggested it was the mere presence of an audience, but Cottrell (1968) suggested that the audience must evaluate the performance. Clearly social factors play a role in sport performance.

An example of behaviour and how the different approaches might explain it

In your AS studies, you will have looked at the Mark Griffiths study on gambling. This takes a cognitive approach to the explanation of gambling. Let's review that and also outline how the other approaches would explain this behaviour.

The cognitive approach would explain gambling in terms of faulty thought processes, irrationalities and cognitive biases. For example, a gambler may irrationally believe that he is better than the machine or casino; that the more you gamble, the more likely is a big win; that the gambling machine is sometimes 'kind' or 'unkind' (anthropomorphism: ascribing human characteristics to an inanimate object). If the gambler could become aware of these faulty thought processes and replace them with rational ones, he would be able to give up gambling.

The physiological approach would explain gambling in terms of the excitement that it generates and specifically the adrenaline release and hit when gambling. This adrenaline hit reinforces the behaviour as it gives a pleasurable sensation (this explanation also draws on positive reinforcement and behaviourism — see later discussion of these).

The social approach would explain gambling in terms of the individual's interactions with other people. Perhaps a gambler has been influenced by his peer group and the behaviour is a matter of conformity. A gambler may identify with others who gamble more than with other people (e.g. family, friends) in his life.

The individual differences approach would consider whether gamblers have some profile of personality traits which is different from that of the non-gambling population. Perhaps gamblers are more sensation-seeking, are greater risk-takers, or have an 'addictive personality'. A psychologist working within the individual differences approach might try to measure gamblers' personalities using psychometric tests.

The developmental approach might try to trace a link between early childhood experiences and behaviour later in life. Perhaps gamblers had some sort of emotional deprivation in childhood and crave excitement as a (dysfunctional) way of trying to make up for the lack of emotional satisfaction. Possibly, early experiences of 'gambling' at innocent activities in childhood (e.g. the school fete raffle) were rewarded by winning (see later discussion of operant conditioning and behaviourism).

Summary

After studying this section, you should be able to define, explain, evaluate (give strengths and weaknesses of) and apply examples from the specification of:
- the cognitive approach
- the physiological approach
- the individual differences approach
- the developmental approach
- the social approach

Perspectives in psychology

What is a perspective, and how does it differ from an approach? Usually, a perspective is more a way of explaining behaviour according to certain principles, concepts and ideas, whereas the approaches listed in the specification refer more to *areas* of research interest (regardless of the perspective adopted). The following sections discuss the behaviourist and psychodynamic perspectives in turn.

The behaviourist perspective

In behaviourist terms, learning is not just something you do at school. All our experience in life leads to some kind of learning (take the simple example of a young child learning through painful experience that it is a bad idea to touch kettles). One of the main assumptions of the behaviourist perspective is that all behaviour is learnt through experience. There are three sub-strands of behaviourism: classical conditioning theory, operant conditioning theory and social learning theory. These will be discussed in turn.

Classical conditioning theory (Pavlov)

We learn through association. For example, we learn a phobia from association with another bad experience. One famous case study is that of Watson and Rayner's Little Albert. Little Albert was shown a white rat. Every time he saw the white rat, the experimenters made a loud bang. He learnt to associate white rats with fear and so acquired a phobic response. Classical conditioning theory has terms for each of the features involved:

(1) Unconditioned stimulus: this is the thing which 'naturally' always produces the same automatic (instinctive or reflexive) response. In other words, you do not need to learn about this — it is part of our biological make-up to respond to this stimulus in a certain way. The following are examples of things which could function as an unconditioned stimulus:
- pleasant-smelling food — by nature, animals will salivate in response
- a loud noise — all animals will make a 'startle' reaction to a loud noise
- pain — many animals will respond to pain in a negative way, for example by reflexive recoiling from the source of pain

(2) Unconditioned response: this is the 'natural', automatic response to the unconditioned stimulus. For example, the unconditioned stimulus of food will result in the unconditioned response of salivating; the unconditioned stimulus of a sudden loud noise will result in the unconditioned response of a startle reaction.

(3) Conditioned stimulus: this is the thing which a person (or animal) learns to react to. It is usually something which is quite 'neutral' — prior to any learning experience it would produce no reaction. It becomes conditioned (learnt) through repeated association with an unconditioned stimulus.

(4) Conditioned response: after the conditioned stimulus has been associated with the unconditioned stimulus, the conditioned response is the same as the unconditioned response.

If we take the example of Little Albert learning a startle (and phobic) response to a white rat, we can represent his process of learning as in Figure 12.

The **behaviourist perspective** focuses on observable behaviour rather than mental concepts and explains behaviour in terms of learning.

Figure 12

When Pavlov originally 'discovered' the mechanism of classical conditioning, he was working with dogs in a laboratory. It was an almost incidental observation. He noticed that, over time, the dogs would start salivating (CR) when they heard a bell ring (even if they could not see or smell food), because they had associated the ringing of a bell (CS) with food (UCS). Thus, the dogs had been 'conditioned' into responding in a certain way to the otherwise neutral stimulus of a bell. Pavlov, as a good scientist, investigated and systematically researched this process, and this led to his theory of classical conditioning.

Operant conditioning theory (Skinner)

Operant conditioning involves a different process of learning. The process is not association, but **reinforcement**. Operant conditioning theory describes how we learn through the *consequences* of our behaviour. In simple terms: if the consequences of a behaviour are good, we are more likely to repeat that behaviour; if the consequences of a behaviour are neutral, we are less likely to repeat that behaviour.

Think of a small child called Fred. Fred is having a tantrum in a shop because he wants his mother to buy him a cuddly toy. According to operant conditioning, the consequences of Fred's behaviour (the tantrum) will determine the likelihood of Fred having a tantrum on another occasion. If his mother decides to stop the tantrum by buying him the toy, she is unwittingly giving the child a **reward** for his behaviour. Thus a tantrum is **positively reinforced** and so is more likely to occur again. If the mother decides to ignore the behaviour entirely, the tantrum behaviour is not reinforced.

However, the mother may react to the behaviour in a different way, such as shouting at or even smacking the child. This is punishment and should mean that the behaviour is less likely to appear again in the future. However, according to Skinner, punishment may actually, unwittingly, sometimes reinforce the behaviour, as the child has got some attention. It might not be the kind of attention he wanted, but it is attention nevertheless and can act as a positive reinforcer.

There is also a different kind of reinforcement — **negative reinforcement** (this is not to be confused with punishment). Negative reinforcement is a process whereby behaviour is reinforced by *avoiding something negative*. Let's say that Fred has done something naughty and knows he is going to be scolded by his mother. He suddenly bursts into tears and says he is really sorry. His mother takes pity and the scolding is now avoided. This avoidance of the scolding reinforces Fred's remorseful behaviour. According to operant conditioning, Fred is more likely to display this remorseful behaviour again in the future.

Figure 13 illustrates operant conditioning processes.

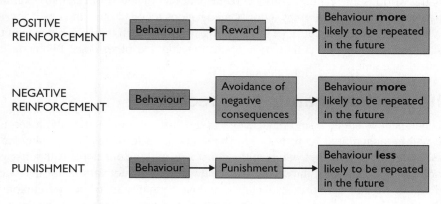

Figure 13

Even though Skinner was first developing this theory of operant conditioning more than 60 years ago, it is difficult to avoid even now. In popular television programmes such as *Supernanny* and *Dog Borstal*, you can see these behaviourist principles being implemented to try to improve and shape behaviour.

Social learning theory

You will have encountered social learning theory in the Bandura core study at AS. According to Bandura, we do not learn only through our own direct experience of the consequences of our behaviour. We also learn through observing other people's behaviour (and the consequences they receive). This was neatly demonstrated in the Bobo doll study, where children were more likely to display new behaviours that they had learnt from observing another person. This imitative learning can work in conjunction with operant conditioning principles too — so that if we see someone else being rewarded for a particular behaviour, we are even more likely to imitate it.

Social learning is a very important way for humans to learn. It explains how we can learn from each other — we do not have to find everything out for ourselves, but can observe other people and adopt their strategies. In a way, it seems obvious — of course, if we have never seen a spade before, and then see someone using it, we are now able to imitate that behaviour. Nevertheless, social learning theory has high explanatory power. It contributes to the debate about television violence as well as helping to explain a variety of everyday behaviours.

Further elaboration of social learning theory seems to show that there are some factors which increase the likelihood of a behaviour being imitated. For example, a more esteemed or high-status model is more likely to be imitated.

A strength and weakness of the behaviourist perspective

- The behaviourist perspective is at the more scientific end of psychology, with its emphases on manipulation and empirical data collection (especially through

The **psychodynamic perspective** emphasises the role of the unconscious mind: the id, ego and superego, and the influence that childhood experiences have on our future lives.

observation). It has been used to explain, understand and treat a huge variety of behavioural and psychological problems. Thus, many applications have arisen out of behaviourism.

- Because behaviourism refuses to acknowledge how we think, how we make sense of the world, some explanations it provides are incomplete. Consider, for example, two people who are bitten by a dog. One develops a dog phobia and one does not. Why? It is probably because of the differing ways in which they make sense of the situation, the cognitions they have about the dog and other dogs. Behaviourism fails to account for this.

The psychodynamic perspective

This perspective stems from Freud's work in the early part of the twentieth century. You will be acquainted with this from the study of Little Hans and his phobias of horses. Freud distinguishes between the conscious and unconscious. Our conscious mind — the part of our mind where we are aware of our motivations for behaviour and which we can verbalise explicitly — is just a small part of our psychological make-up. It is our unconscious mind — where the motivations for behaviour are often complex and related in some way to sex, and largely hidden from our conscious minds — that is actually the real driving force.

One of the main ideas of Freud is the 'tripartite' personality — that there are three aspects of self:

(1) The **id**. We are born with this. It is the 'me, me, me and only me' instinct. It is the 'I want...' part of our personality. I want a cuddle, I want some food, I want a drink, I want to go to sleep, I want to cry: all of that from a baby. As an adult, the list of desires only increases: I want a cuddle, some food and a drink, and then a sleep, but I also want to be the best at my job, to be admired by everyone, to have the latest Audi car and to be with that person... and to kick that other person. Some of our desires may not be very sociable or positive, but that will not stop the id wanting them.

(2) The **superego**. This is the part of personality we develop during the phallic stage as we learn to identify with the same-sex parent and internalise their moral code. The superego is rather a killjoy for the id, as the superego wants to regulate behaviour to make it acceptable. It is concerned with what a person *should* do. Thus, while the id might want you to pick up the £10 note the previous diners have left on the restaurant table as a tip for the waiter, the superego knows this is unacceptable. There is a lot of conflict between the superego and the id, as their operating principles ('I should' versus 'I want') are diametrically opposed.

(3) The **ego**. This part of the personality has the job of mediating between the id and the superego and trying to keep both aspects relatively 'happy' but also in check.

Freud had a theory of psychosexual development, describing a number of stages during childhood. According to Freud, each stage has a particular (predetermined) focus of 'sexual gratification' and it is important that the conflict is resolved so that the child can continue into adulthood without any dysfunctional behaviour. The stages include the oral stage (age 0–1), with the focus on sucking and later biting, and the anal stage (age 1–3), with the focus on expelling and retaining faeces. Through control of these bodily functions, the child obtains approval and love from parents and also learns to deal with authority.

Finally, another important concept from the psychodynamic perspective is that of **ego-defence mechanisms**. These are strategies that the ego deploys in order to try to protect or minimise the psychological discomfort from the conflict generated between the superego and the id. Here are some examples of ego-defence mechanisms:

- Repression: this involves forcing an unpleasant or threatening thought or memory from the conscious to the unconscious.
- Displacement: if a person cannot express his or her feelings openly to the real person or target, he or she may displace them onto another target (e.g. slamming the door rather than having a big argument with your mother).

Knowledge check 26

Give an assumption of the psychodynamic perspective using an example.

A strength and weakness of the psychodynamic perspective

- This perspective often gives us unusual insights by suggesting that not all behaviours are what they seem, and that even our own motives might be unknown to us because they reside in the depths of the unconscious. Thus, ideas of 'Freudian slips', 'death wishes' and so on seem to offer interesting (and often entertaining) explanations of behaviour.
- Because of the very nature of this perspective's understanding of the human conscious and unconscious, it presents a very disempowered view of humans: we do not even understand ourselves *and* all our behaviour has been determined by prior experience.

Examiner tip

Think beyond the immediate issue again. What methods, debates and issues apply to the psychodynamic perspective? Is it reductionist? Is it deterministic? What else might it be?

An example of behaviour and how the different perspectives might explain it

How would these perspectives explain our everyday example of gambling?

Operant conditioning theory would explain it in terms of positive reinforcement. For an individual gambler, his or her reinforcement history would explain it. Of course, gambling is in itself highly reinforcing. Skinner, when experimenting with pigeons and rats in his 'Skinner box', found that different patterns of rewarding behaviour with food had differential effects in terms of the likelihood of repeating the behaviour. For instance, a bird's behaviour of pecking at a lever was more strongly reinforced when it received food with moderate frequency but in an unpredictable pattern (e.g. roughly 1 in every 10 pecks rather than exactly 1 in every 10 pecks). This unpredictable pattern of reinforcement is exactly a typical gambler's experience of winning money on a roulette wheel or fruit machine. Operant conditioning can also explain gambling through other reinforcers, such as excitement, mental stimulation and attention from other people.

Social learning theory would suggest that a gambler may have learnt the behaviour from observing someone else model it. Possibly a parent gambled during the gambler's childhood, or a friend or colleague was observed gambling during adulthood. The higher the status of the model, and the greater the reward he or she was observed to receive, the greater the likelihood of the behaviour being imitated.

Classical conditioning would suggest that a gambler has learnt to associate gambling with a positive unconditioned stimulus — for example, an adrenaline rush. Repeated associations (co-occurrences) of gambling and experiencing an adrenaline rush lead to the conditioned response of feeling excited and high.

The psychodynamic perspective would explain gambling in terms of subconscious desires and motivations. Gambling is a risky business and is perhaps an expression of a subconscious death wish. Alternatively the psychodynamic perspective might explain gambling in terms of one or more ego-defence mechanisms such as:

- denial — typically gamblers find the idea of losing anxiety-provoking, so they deny this distinct possibility by refusing to consciously acknowledge this as the most likely outcome
- displacement — rather than investing emotional energy (which in Freud's view would mean 'sexual energy') and impulses into something perceived as threatening, gamblers re-direct it to a safer outlet. Instead of focusing attention upon a loved one who may reject them, they focus on something less threatening, such as gambling. (Most spouses of addictive gamblers perceive that the gambling is a replacement or competitor for spending time with them.)

Examiner tip
You may be asked to *compare* one perspective with another — a comparison is a *similarity*. You may be asked to *contrast* one perspective with another — a contrast is a *difference*.

We have now looked at a number of different ways of explaining gambling. Which do you think is the most plausible? Which has the most power? Might it be the case that, for any one gambler, a number of these explanations apply, or do you think a single explanation is sufficient? In the next two sections we will look at debates and issues in psychology and this will help us further understand, evaluate and compare the merits of the different perspectives and approaches.

Summary

After studying this section, you should be able to define, explain, evaluate (give strengths and weaknesses of) and apply examples from the specification to:

- the behaviourist perspective
- the psychodynamic perspective

Debates in psychology

The debates to be discussed are as follows:

- determinism and free will
- reductionism and holism
- nature–nurture
- ethnocentrism
- psychology as science
- individual and situational explanations
- the usefulness of psychological research

For each debate a description will be given, and strengths and weaknesses (or arguments for and against) discussed, followed (where applicable) by two or more examples from AS core studies or A2 options. It is also important for you to think of your own examples.

Determinism and free will

Determinism is the view that we do not have much control over our behaviour or our destiny, but are controlled by factors such as our biology or genetics, or by the reinforcements we are given.

Determinism represents the view that all behaviours, all mental acts (e.g. thoughts, judgements, decisions), are determined by factors out of our control. Free will represents the view that our behaviours and mental acts all come about as a result of our own choice and volition — that is, we can exercise our own free will.

Take the example of suicide:

- Determinist explanations might say that this could be **predicted** through a number of possible factors (perhaps in combination), such as a person's upbringing, a genetic or biochemical disposition to feeling hopeless, faulty thought patterns which focus on negativity, and social isolation. (These determinist explanations can come from any approach — physiological, developmental, cognitive and so on.) In this view, the person did not actively choose to commit suicide (even if the person thinks that he or she did); instead, his or her action was a predictable conclusion to a long chain of events and occurrences.
- A free will explanation would emphasise that the person who committed suicide chose that course of action of his or her own free will and that he or she might equally have chosen *not* to commit suicide.

There is a milder form of determinism, called 'soft determinism', which says that, although as humans we do have choices to make and can exercise free will, these choices are often constrained (or determined) by factors. Indeed, some choices are more likely than others, and this is determined by, say, previous experiences.

Strengths of determinism

- The emphasis on cause and effect means that determinist explanations make the world more understandable and predictable. This suggests that it could be worthwhile in trying to change certain things (e.g. education systems or child-rearing practices) because it could have positive effects.
- Determinism is the purpose and goal of science: to explain the causes of things (of behaviour, in the case of psychology). This makes it more acceptable to society, with its explanations, scientific basis and objectivity.

Weaknesses of determinism

- It does not allow (especially in *hard* determinism) for free will. A hard determinist would say that free will is an illusion — we *think* we have choice, but it is just an illusion.
- Determinism can never fully explain behaviour because behaviour may be far too complex. It is often reductionist.

Examples of determinism

(1) A2 option: Wikström (2003) is determinist in that he suggests particular risk factors which determine if someone will become a criminal. These include: propensity-induced factors (i.e. personality characteristics), lifestyle-dependent factors (high-risk) and situationally limited factors (some situations, such as drug use, promote further criminal offences).
(2) A2 option: the work of humanists such as Rogers and Maslow underlines the importance of free will in education.

Reductionism and holism

The **reductionist** view of the world looks for explanations which break things down into smaller constituent parts. This can be powerful, but sometimes provides

---

Examiner tip

Just like approaches and perspectives, you should know at least two examples from psychological research of each debate. Again, all the examiner tips that were made about approaches and perspectives apply to debates in exactly the same way.

Knowledge check 27

Give an example of environmental determinism and an example of biological determinism.

Examiner tip

Two examples are given here from A2 options. Can you give two examples from the AS course?

Reductionism is the process of explaining complex psychological phenomena by reducing them to their component parts. This is the opposite of **holism**, where the total is more than the sum of the parts.

an explanation which is simplistic, ignoring other important aspects or factors. A **holistic** view looks at a person as whole, or perhaps looks at a complex of factors which together might explain a particular behaviour.

Strengths of reductionism

- It helps us to understand the world, as a fundamental way of understanding is to analyse, break things down into component parts, test them and then build them back up again. This is important in studying the world and humans in a scientific way.
- In theory it is easier to study one component rather than several interacting components. If one component is isolated and others are controlled then the study is more objective and scientifically acceptable.

Weaknesses of reductionism

- Because it can isolate factors, it does not always give a proper, valid and full account of a behaviour (see comments on SSRIs below).
- Components may be difficult to isolate and so manipulate. Any behaviour may not be meaningful if it is studied in isolation from the wider social context.

Examples of reductionism

(1) A2 option: SSRIs (selective serotonin reuptake inhibitors) are used to treat depression. The causes of depression are multiple and wide-ranging, and in any one person are likely to involve a confluence of factors. Thus, treating only one aspect of the depression (the symptoms), rather than some of the more complex psychological underlying causes, is a simplistic and reductionist approach.

(2) A2 option (Raine 1997): although Raine's work is sometimes said to be reductionist (because he is 'only' looking at areas of the brain), this is probably mistaken. In his research, he outlines quite complex models of causation for aggression, called 'bio-psycho-social pathways' — which, as the name suggests, explain aggression in terms of a combination of brain abnormality with psychological and social experience, including aspects such as educational experience and interpersonal cognition.

Nature–nurture

This debate centres on whether particular behaviours are mainly, or entirely, innate (inborn or genetically determined, i.e. **nature**) or whether they are acquired through experience or the influence of the environment (**nurture**). Interestingly, both nature and nurture views of humans are determinist, as neither gives scope for free will. Increasingly, people acknowledge that many behaviours come about through a mixture of inborn predispositions and environmental experience (i.e. a mix of nature and nurture).

Strengths of nature–nurture

- The distinction can help us identify behaviours that are inherited or learnt, or allow us to consider the relative contributions of inheritance and learning.
- It can be valuable to discover that some behaviours are due to nature and not to 'inappropriate' upbringing by parents.

Knowledge check 28

Why are both the nature and nurture arguments reductionist?

Nature in this sense refers to the part of us that is inherited and genetic, as distinct from **nurture**, which refers to all influences after our birth (i.e. experience).

Weaknesses of nature–nurture

- It is simplistic to divide explanations into either nature or nurture, as the two often combine in complex ways to influence behaviour.
- Discovering that a particular behaviour or capacity (e.g. intelligence) is inherited may lead some to assume many more behaviours are inherited and to fail to consider the effects of the environment.

Examples of nature–nurture

(1) Core study (nurture): the study by Bandura et al. supports social learning theory, proposed by Bandura (detailed earlier in the discussion of the behaviourist perspective, see page 53).

(2) A2 option (nature): Gottesman and Shields (1972) examined the records of 57 schizophrenics between 1948 and 1964. They found concordance rates (the probability of a twin having schizophrenia if the other twin has it) as follows: monozygotic (genetically identical) twins 42% and dizygotic (non-identical) twins 9%. This provided evidence of a genetic link for schizophrenia.

Ethnocentrism

There are two forms of **ethnocentrism**. The first, more brutal, form of ethnocentrism is an explicit belief that one's own group (e.g. ethnic, social, cultural) is the most important. The other form of ethnocentrism is a softer version — the idea that, as individuals and groups, we find it hard to think outside our own cultural experience, so we just unquestioningly assume that the way things happen in our own culture is the way things happen in all other cultures. This means that, in research, psychologists might design research or draw conclusions in a way that makes sense or applies to their own cultural group, but may have little meaning to other cultural groups. This could be because the sample in the study reflects only one culture. It may also be that the questions asked, the task given or the interpretation of the results assume a particular cultural background.

Strengths of studying ethnocentrism

- Arguably, ethnocentrism is the root cause of prejudice and discrimination. Research on ethnocentrism (such as Tajfel's famous in-group out-group studies) helps us to understand the mechanisms by which discrimination arises.
- By understanding the mechanisms of ethnocentrism, we should be more able to address them in order to improve society, so that it can become more socially cohesive.
- Researchers need to be wary of assuming that their culture is superior or the norm, otherwise there is a danger that their research or tests will be biased. For example, early IQ tests have been shown to be biased towards white, middle-class Americans and against black Americans. The ethnocentrism in these tests had serious consequences for the test-takers (Gould 1986).

Weaknesses of studying ethnocentrism

- No weakness — greater awareness of our own ethnocentric tendencies (whether overt or implicit) can only be a good thing as an individual in society or as a researcher.

Knowledge check 29

Why are both the nature and nurture arguments deterministic?

The term **ethnocentrism** comes from the words 'ethnos', meaning 'nation' in modern Greek, and 'kentro', which means 'centre'.

Psychology as a science

There is a long-standing debate about whether or not psychology is genuinely a science.

Arguments for psychology as a science

- It is a research-based subject with investigation at its core.
- Psychology uses the scientific method in its investigations: it is carried out through genuine experimentation (manipulation of IVs), using many controls.
- Like other sciences, psychology has theories. Theories generate hypotheses and these are tested empirically, so that the theories are tested and refined.

Arguments against psychology as a science

- Psychology's subject matter is humans. They cannot be investigated in the same way as the subject matter of, say, chemistry or physics — because people are aware of being investigated and interact with the researchers, and this alters their behaviour.
- Much of what psychology is interested in — the mind, motivation, emotion and so on — is not open to genuine scientific and empirical research because it is not actually *observable*. Psychologists only guess or infer what is happening, rather than collecting direct empirical data.
- There is no single unifying theory or framework (or paradigm) in psychology, as there is in other sciences. This may be because psychology is still a relatively young subject, and is still in a state of 'pre-science', but perhaps it will never be a genuine science.
- Much material which is called 'psychology' is clearly not science (e.g. humanism, Freudian theories).

Discussion

Which set of arguments do you think is stronger? On the positive side, science tends to have 'high status' and to be given more credibility and more funding. On the negative side, some argue that adopting a more scientific approach would lead to a neglect or downgrading of interesting areas of psychology which are not really subject to scientific scrutiny.

Individual and situational explanations

This is another debate which runs through psychology. An **individual** (**dispositional**) explanation for an event will look to some feature or characteristic of the person, whereas a **situational** explanation will look at the wider context — the social group, the physical environment. For example, suppose a small boy is violent towards his classmates. Is this because he has a violent personality (individual explanation)? Or is it because he is provoked by his classmates, his home life encourages violent behaviour, or all the boys are violent and he is just fitting in (situational explanations)?

Strengths of individual and situational explanations

- If we can discover which behaviours are individually determined and which are situationally determined, such findings may be useful for society.
- Discovering that behaviour may involve a complex interaction between individual and situational factors opens up new directions for further study.

Knowledge check 30

Briefly debate the argument for and against psychology being a science.

Examiner tip

What psychological research do you think is more scientific and what research do you think is less scientific? Are some approaches more scientific than others? Are some perspectives more scientific than others?

Individual and situational explanations refer to the way that we describe the cause of a behaviour as being due to something in that person (**individual** or **dispositional**) or as a response to the situation that they are in (**situational**).

Weaknesses of individual and situational explanations

- It can be difficult to separate the effects of a situation from the disposition of a participant.
- How can situations be investigated? If investigated in a laboratory there is low ecological validity; if investigated in a natural setting the situation may be difficult to control.
- Rather than individual or situational factors being exclusive alternatives, there may be a complex interaction between the two.

Examples of individual and situational explanations

(1) Core study by Rosenhan (situational): abnormality is not a property of the person, but perceived in someone because of the situation and context. Thus, normal behaviour in a mental hospital may appear abnormal (e.g. waiting at the canteen was seen as 'oral acquisitive behaviour').

(2) A2 option study (individual): Gottesman and Shields' study appears to establish a link between genes and schizophrenia. This is an individual type of explanation because the cause of the behaviour is rooted *within* the individual, rather than in any aspect of the environment or situation. Oruc et al. (1998) would claim the same for the cause of affective disorders and Ost (1992) for anxiety disorders.

Knowledge check 31

What is meant by a 'dispositional' explanation of behaviour? Give an example from your AS course of a *situational* explanation and give an example from your A2 course of a *dispositional* explanation.

The usefulness of psychological research

This is really more an issue than a debate. In psychology, some research is clearly much more useful than other research — some research naturally lends itself to real-life applications (e.g. advice on the best way to raise and educate children, health promotion, diagnosing and treating mental illnesses). Other research is less clearly useful, though this need not mean that it will never be useful — it may just be that we cannot see the application *yet*.

Strengths of useful research

- If research is useful then it can be of benefit to society; it can improve the world in which we live.
- If research is useful then it enhances the value of psychology as a subject.

Weaknesses of useful research

- Any study must be ethical — participants should give informed consent and not be deceived. However, a study may need to be unethical to be really useful.
- Any study should be ecologically valid. Studies conducted in a laboratory may not be useful as they are low in ecological validity.
- Any study should use a representative sample and be generalisable. Useful research should apply worldwide so there is no ethnocentrism.
- Any study should not be reductionist; it should not only apply in isolation from other behaviours but in various contexts.

Knowledge check 32

Psychologists want their research to be useful. Outline three methodological problems that psychologists should address if they want their research to be useful.

Examples of useful and 'less useful' research

(1) Core study by Loftus and Palmer: this is extremely useful research that has impacted on police and court processes. It helped to establish that eyewitness testimony is not always completely accurate and so should not be used, on its own, to convict someone. In addition, because this research demonstrated that leading questions after the event can alter memory, police training in interviewing techniques encourages police to avoid the use of leading questions.

(2) A2 option: Schwartz and Barsky (1977) look at 'home advantage' in sports teams. If it is determined exactly what that advantage is, then 'away' teams may be able to perform much better.

(3) Core study by Savage-Rumbaugh on chimpanzees: it is difficult to see how this research could have a positive impact on human lives. However, perhaps it is important for us to understand how intelligent other animals are: it is a reminder that humans are not the only sentient beings on the planet and that we should have more regard for other species. Although it is not *useful*, it is certainly *influential*.

Summary

After studying this section, you should be able to define, explain, evaluate (give strengths and weaknesses of) and apply examples from the specification to **debates** about:
- determinism
- reductionism
- nature–nurture
- ethnocentrism
- psychology as a science
- individual and situational explanations
- the usefulness of psychological research

Issues in psychology

Two of the issues listed in this section of the specification have already been covered in the discussion of research methods: ecological validity and ethical issues. This section covers the remaining two issues: longitudinal and snapshot studies, and qualitative and quantitative data. For each one, a description will be given, and strengths and weaknesses discussed, followed by two or more examples from AS core studies or A2 options. It is also important for you to think of your own examples.

Longitudinal and snapshot studies

A longitudinal study takes place over a period of time, usually following one or more participants throughout the period (or visiting them at regular intervals) to monitor changes. A snapshot study takes place just at one point in time, and so gives a one-off picture (hence 'snapshot') of the behaviour which is being studied.

Strengths of longitudinal studies
- They can show change and development in an individual.
- They give a fuller, and probably more accurate, picture of the behaviour in general.

Drawbacks of longitudinal studies
- They may be costly.
- It can be difficult to track participants over a long period of time — for example, they may move house or may not want to continue participating. Thus, longitudinal studies tend to lose participants as they go along. This is called 'participant attrition'.

Examples of longitudinal studies

(1) Core study: Thigpen and Cleckley monitored Eve White over a period of approximately 14 months. During that time, they recorded the emergence of Eve Black and later Jane, how Eve responded to hypnotherapy and the changes in her life.

(2) Core study: Savage-Rumbaugh et al. monitored the chimpanzees, especially Kanzi, for 17 months (from 30 to 47 months). As well as monitoring how Kanzi was reared and exposed to lexigrams, they kept a complete record of his utterances during that period. This meant they could study his vocabulary acquisition pattern and how he combined words to form 'sentences'.

(3) A2 option: Farrington et al.'s study of delinquent development involved a longitudinal survey of more than 400 8- and 9-year-olds who were born in the mid-1950s. By monitoring them throughout their lives, the researchers have found that the crime level peaked around age 17. Some were persistent and chronic offenders (7%), while others were occasional offenders. The chronic offenders were more likely to have a convicted parent, a delinquent sibling and a young mother, and to come from a big family. By age 48, the majority had given up crime.

Knowledge check 33

What is meant by the term 'longitudinal study'? Give one drawback or problem with longitudinal studies and give two examples where this problem did not apply.

Strengths of snapshot studies

- They are a quick way to collect data, especially if long-term development is not relevant.
- They can be useful in obtaining preliminary evidence before getting locked into expensive and time-consuming longitudinal work.
- They may give an indication of how people are likely to respond or behave.
- Data are likely to be quantitative (i.e. in the form of numbers), making statistical analysis possible.

Weaknesses of snapshot studies

- It is not possible to study how behaviour may change over time (development); one cannot see the long-term effectiveness or impact of a treatment or of exposure to certain stimuli.
- Behaviour recorded is limited to that time, place and culture.
- Data are likely to be quantitative and the explanation of why a participant behaved in a particular way will not be known.
- One cannot see effects of societal changes on people's psychology.

Examples of snapshot studies

(1) Core study by Bandura et al.: this only shows the children's aggression towards the Bobo doll at one moment in time (and just a few minutes after watching the acts of aggression) and so it is a snapshot study. It would have been interesting to see whether the imitative acts of aggression were displayed by the children after 1 day, 1 week, 1 month and so on. This would help us understand whether watching aggressive acts has a short-term or long-term effect on behaviour.

(2) A2 option: Janis and Feshbach on fear arousal. This study showed that giving high fear information about lack of dental hygiene actually had a negative impact. However, they only asked the participants immediately after the information had been given and it would have been interesting to see if, in the longer term, the high fear arousal would be beneficial.

Examiner tip

Think more widely again. Can we judge the effectiveness (or usefulness) of something if the study is snapshot?

Quantitative and qualitative data

Quantitative data are numeric (i.e. in the form of numbers). Examples of quantitative data in research include a score recorded for each participant, the time taken to complete a task, or the number of people in each condition who displayed a particular behaviour. **Qualitative data** are in the form of words. Examples include descriptions of events, quotes from participants, or descriptions of participants' responses to a task.

Often, studies contain a mixture of quantitative and qualitative data. Milgram's study obtained quantitative data in terms of the percentage of participants who continued to each shock level. However, it also obtained a lot of qualitative data about participants' behaviour while administering the (fake) shocks, including descriptions of them shaking and sweating, and records of what they said to the experimenter in the room.

Strengths of quantitative data

- Quantitative data allow statistics to be applied and comparisons to be made easily.
- Quantitative data are 'objective' and more 'scientific'.

Weaknesses of quantitative data

- Numbers are often produced in isolation from interpretation (possibly through a snapshot study).
- To analyse people as nothing more than numbers is reductionist.
- Using quantitative data ignores any subjective element — the reason *why* a behaviour occurred.

Strengths of qualitative data

- Data can be in depth, rich in detail and insightful, and therefore not reductionist.
- Data can help us understand why people behave in a particular way.

Weaknesses of qualitative data

- There may be problems of interpretation. Words and descriptions are more subjective than numbers and are more open to bias and misinterpretation.
- It may be much more difficult to make statistical comparisons.
- The data may be more prone to researcher bias as information that best fits a hypothesis could be selected.
- Participants may give socially desirable answers. Participants may want to look good for the experimenter.

Examples of quantitative and qualitative data

(1) Qualitative data were gathered by Freud, and by Thigpen and Cleckley through the Rorschach test.

(2) Quantitative data were gathered by Loftus and Palmer through the estimations of speed in experiment 1 and whether participants answered 'yes' or 'no' in experiment 2. Samuel and Bryant also gathered quantitative data in the number of errors made (out of 4) by the children in the conservation tasks.

Quantitative data are data that focus on numbers and frequencies rather than on meaning or experience.

Qualitative data are data that describe meaning and experience in the form of words rather than providing numerical values for behaviour.

Examiner tip

Know examples of studies that use just quantitative data and know examples of studies that use just qualitative data. Don't forget studies that use both.

Knowledge check 34

Thinking about your research design, give three reasons why quantitative data might be better than qualitative data.

Knowledge check 35

Using a core study as an example, give one disadvantage of not gathering qualitative data.

(3) Qualitative and quantitative data were gathered in the Dement and Kleitman sleep and dreaming study. Quantitative data consisted of the number of dreams recalled during REM or NREM sleep, and qualitative data consisted of the subjective reports of dream contents, such as playing basketball and throwing tomatoes.

Knowledge check 36

What is meant by qualitative data? Give one advantage of qualitative data.

After studying this section, you should be able to define, explain, evaluate (give strengths and weaknesses of) and apply examples from the specification to the **issues** of:

- snapshot and longitudinal data
- qualitative and quantitative data

Summary

Questions & Answers

Examination guidance

The Approaches and Research Methods in Psychology examination paper G544 lasts for 1½ hours. Section A is on research methods. Section B is on approaches, perspectives, methods, issues and debates. You must answer *all* the questions in Section A and *one* question in Section B.

The advice on the front of the question paper is very sensible and should be followed: Read each question carefully and make sure you know what you have to do before starting your answer.

This section of the guide contains a sample Section A passage and questions, and one sample Section B question, along with two student answers and examiner's comments for each.

Section A is on research methods. It asks you to design a practical project. Your starting point will be a short scene-setting passage with some context. There will then be a series of possible research questions which could be investigated. You need to choose *one* of these and design a research activity to investigate it. The guidance is that this should be a project which, at least notionally, you could conduct yourself. Perhaps more importantly, you should design a project which will help you answer all the questions in Section A. Therefore, before you start answering question 1, read *all* the Section A questions. You can then, in rough, plan your project with these in mind before going on to answer the questions.

Section B is on approaches, perspectives, methods, issues and debates. Section B asks you to choose from one of two questions, each of which will be on a different approach, perspective, method, issue or debate. Each question will have sub-parts. Each question is allocated the same number of marks, and each will have the same number of question sub-parts (probably five, (a) to (e)), and will require you to display your knowledge and understanding of an approach, perspective, method, issue or debate, drawing on examples from elsewhere in your psychology course.

Each section is worth 40 marks, so you should divide your time equally between them. As the examination paper lasts for 90 minutes, spend 45 minutes on Section A and 45 minutes on Section B.

Candidates often finish writing ahead of time, but there is no prize for finishing first. On the other hand, make sure you do not run out of time. Try testing yourself so that you know exactly how much you can write in the time allowed.

OCR examinations are now marked online. This means that at the start of the examination you will be given a combined question-and-answer booklet. You must write only within the lines provided for each question because if you don't the pages will not scan correctly and the examiner may not receive your whole answer. If you wish to write more for an answer than the lines given, there are additional lined sheets at the back of the booklet for 'overflow'. However, you must indicate clearly within the first part of the answer that you have continued on the additional page to ensure that the examiner knows to look for the additional part of your response.

The table below summarises the mark allocation, time allocation and recommended length of answer for the Unit G544 examination.

Section	Mark allocation	Time spent planning	Time spent writing	Time spent on section	Amount of writing
Section A	40 marks	10 min	35 min	45 min	4 sides of A4*
Section B	40 marks	10 min	35 min	45 min	4 sides of A4†
Totals	80 marks	20 min	70 min	90 min	7–9 sides of A4

* For Section A, you should not need to write more than 3–4 sides of A4. The expected length of the answer is indicated by the number of lines given in the question-and-answer booklet. The art of planning a good investigation is to keep it quite tight, focused and logical. If you are writing considerably more, you may be trying to do too much in one investigation.

† For Section B, if you can write more than 4 sides (and it is relevant), then do so. Again, the expected length of the answer is indicated in the question-and-answer booklet.

Assessment objectives

The three assessment objectives examined in this unit are summarised below.

AO1: knowledge and understanding

You should be able to:
  a recognise, recall and show understanding of scientific knowledge
  b select, organise and communicate relevant information in a variety of forms

AO1 assesses what you know about psychology and whether you understand it. Examination questions here will ask you, for example, to outline or describe a design or procedure of a project, or to outline the developmental psychology approach or the free will and determinism debate.

AO2: application of knowledge and understanding

You should be able to:
  a analyse and evaluate scientific knowledge and processes
  b apply scientific knowledge and processes to unfamiliar situations, including those related to issues
  c assess the validity, reliability and credibility of scientific information

AO2 assesses your evaluation skills, and examination questions will ask you to discuss, evaluate or compare.

AO3: science in practice

You should be able to:
  a demonstrate ethical, safe and skilful practical techniques and processes, selecting appropriate qualitative and quantitative methods

b make, record and communicate reliable and valid observations and measurements with appropriate precision and accuracy

c analyse, interpret, explain and evaluate the methodology, results and impact of your own and others' experimental and investigative activities in a variety of ways

AO3 makes up a large part of Approaches and Research Methods in Psychology, because the very nature of the unit is science in practice.

Examiner's comments

Examiner's comments on the questions are preceded by the icon ⓔ and offer tips on what you need to do to gain full marks. Examiner's comments on the answers are preceded by the icon ⓔ and indicate where credit is due. In the weaker answers, they also point out areas for improvement, specific problems and common errors, such as lack of clarity, weak or non-existent development, irrelevance, misinterpretation of the question and mistaken meanings of terms.

Section A

Read the passage below.

History is full of conmen, hustlers, scammers and deceivers. But of course, in order for there to be conmen, there have to be people who are willing to be 'taken in' and deceived. In some ways, it is always surprising when we find out that people were taken in.

A couple of years ago, there was a story in the news of a funny and bizarre scam in Japan. In this country, poodles are quite rare but seen as a status symbol for the young, rich and famous. About 2,000 people were sold 'miniature poodles' for approximately £650 each. In fact they were not poodles or even dogs at all. Instead, they were lambs with their fleece shaved in the same way as poodles. It was only when a famous actress showed viewers a picture of her pet poodle on a television talk show, complaining that her dog 'refused to bark or eat its tinned food', that the scam was exposed. The scam had apparently worked because poodles are quite rare in Japan, and sheep are almost entirely unknown.

More seriously, perhaps, there was the recent case of Bernie Madoff, responsible for the biggest financial fraud in the history of Wall Street. Lots of clever, sophisticated people, who apparently should have known better, invested millions of dollars into his dodgy schemes — and many have now lost those millions. To become a member of the Madoff fund was quite difficult — entry was strictly by invitation only. Clients were recruited from his own friendship groups and members of the same yachting, golf or country club. They all believed that, even when no one else could, Madoff really could invest money and give handsome returns.

Why are humans so easily deceived?
- Can humans accurately judge whether someone is trustworthy from their face?
- Can humans accurately judge whether someone is trustworthy from their body language?
- Are we more likely to be deceived by someone offering us something that is a luxury rather than a necessity?
- Are we more likely to be deceived by someone in our in-group rather than in our out-group?
- Are we more likely to be deceived by someone of the same sex or of the opposite sex?
- Are we more likely to believe a lie when it is something we would like to believe (rather than something we would not like to believe)?
- Are we more likely to believe 'white lies' than big lies?

You are required to design a practical project to investigate one of the above research questions. It must be a repeated measures design experiment.

Answer *all* questions in this section:

(1) State an operationalised hypothesis for your investigation. (3 marks)

ⓔ This question wants a hypothesis (not a null) and it must be operationalised. The proposed project is an experiment, so make sure your hypothesis mentions the IV, DV and whether it is one- or two-tailed.

(2) Describe the procedure for your investigation, making clear how you would measure the dependent variable and giving examples of materials you would use. (13 + 6 marks)

ⓔ This 'big' question is worth 19 marks altogether. This is nearly a quarter of all the marks available on the paper. Examiners will therefore want to see quite a lot put into this question. The 19 marks are split into:

- 13 marks for replicability — with a mark given for each point of detail about sample, procedure, materials, scoring etc.
- 3 marks for 'fitness of purpose' — whether the design of the study matches the research question and is (as this sample question stipulates) a repeated measures design, and is practical and ethical
- 3 marks for quality of design and communication — how well it is explained overall, whether it is clear and coherent

(3) Briefly describe how you would summarise and analyse the data. You should identify which inferential test you would use. (3 marks)

ⓔ Read this question carefully. You have to describe how you would summarise the data and this would involve descriptive statistics such as mean, median, mode, range and a visual display. The question merely asks you to identify the test. It does not ask you to explain why you chose the test.

(4) If, having carried out the inferential statistical analysis, you find that your results have a p value of $p > 0.05$, what would '$p > 0.05$' mean and what would you conclude? (3 marks)

ⓔ Again, there are two parts to this question and you need to ensure that you answer both.

(5) (a) Describe one weakness of the repeated measures design in relation to your investigation. (3 marks)
(b) Suggest one way in which the effects of the weakness could be reduced. (3 marks)

ⓔ There are also two parts to this question, helpfully labelled (a) and (b). Before you start writing, read part (b). Will your part (a) answer allow you to write part (b)? If it won't, change your part (a) answer. For part (a), you need to know what a repeated measures design is and you must relate it to your study rather than just defining what it is. For part (b), you need to make a suggestion. There is no right or wrong answer here, merely a suggestion of what you might do to resolve the weakness. Anything appropriate will score marks.

(6) Briefly discuss the validity of your study. (3 marks)

ⓔ You know what validity is (and hopefully you haven't confused it with reliability), so what about your study: is it measuring what it claims to measure?

(7) Outline one way in which you show awareness of ethical issues in the conduct of your study. (3 marks)

ⓔ The easiest way to show that any study you have done is ethical is to have a sentence or two on standardised instructions. This means that at the outset you ask your participants 'Do you give your consent to take part?' If you have the additional comment 'You have the right to withdraw at any time', you have met two ethical guidelines.

Student A

(1) There will be a significant difference **a** in the rates of deception **b** between males and females **c**.

ⓔ **2/3 marks awarded** The student has a hypothesis (correctly) rather than a null hypothesis. There is inclusion of **a** 'significant difference' and there is the inclusion of some form of **b** DV and **c** IV. However, it is not clear what is meant by 'rates of deception' — it is not precise enough.

(2) I will use a survey to investigate this. I will ask 20 males and 20 females from around my college to take part, so it will be an opportunity sample and the parent population **d** will be college students between 16 and 19 years of age. The questionnaire **e** will ask them questions such as:

What is your sex?

Has anyone deceived you in the last 6 months?

If yes, please give brief details of each occasion, e.g. relationship of person to you and what they deceived you about.

Occasion 1:f

Person: relationship to you _____ male / female _____

What they deceived you about:

Occasion 2:

Person: relationship to you _____ male / female _____

What they deceived you about:

Occasion 3:

Etc. (as above — there will be room to write about up to 10 occasions)

I will approach each possible participant. I will give them a brief outline of the study and tell them it is about being deceived. Then I will ask them if they consent to participate. If they do, I will tell them that they will have the right to withdraw and that they can decide to stop participating at any time. I will also tell them that all of the contents of their questionnaire will be completely anonymous and I will not share them with anybody. I will give them the questionnaire to fill in themselves and an envelope in which to return it to me. I will then analyse the results by making a note of the deceptions and who deceived whom etc.

9/19 marks awarded This 'big' question is worth 19 marks altogether. The 19 marks are split into: 13 marks for replicability, 3 marks for 'fitness of purpose' and 3 marks for quality of design and communication.

Replicability: this student's answer contains some detail in terms of the sample, **d** the parent population, **e** the questionnaire and the details of the main questions. However, there is nothing about the scoring of the questionnaire at this point. (Unfortunately, the student includes this in the *next* question, rather than this one. Note that scoring should be in this question and analysis in the next one.) In order to get more marks, the student could have included more details about recruiting the sample (e.g. from class, the library, the canteen). He could also have said more about whether the questionnaire was timed or not, given to fill out in a classroom or take home. As it stands, marks would be awarded for the example questions, the details given for the sample and the information given to the participants, to total 6 marks.

Fitness for purpose: **f** a questionnaire is quite reasonable in itself, though, at this stage, it is not completely clear to the examiner that the student knows that the study will manage to test one of the proposed research questions or that the design will genuinely be repeated measures as stipulated in this question. There is a strong sense that this student has started writing without really planning how the answer will relate to the criteria stipulated in the resource material. Although the questionnaire has some ethical advantages over a possible experiment, there still remains some ethical doubt: some participants' recollections of deception might be quite painful (e.g. betrayal by girlfriend or boyfriend) and so it might cause some stress. Therefore, with the elements of doubt about the fundamentals of fitting the research question and repeated measures design, the answer merits only 1 mark out of 3 here.

Clarity of design: what is present is clear and coherent, though with some omissions and lack of detail; 2/3 marks here.

(3) I would summarise the data by tallying up number of deceptions for each participant in a table like this:

Participant number g	Number of deceptions by same sex	Number of deceptions by opposite sex
1	4	6
2	5	0
3	1	1
4	3	4
Etc.		
Total h	19	15

This would give an overall view of whether people are more likely to be deceived by people of the same sex or opposite sex. It is a repeated measures design because each participant is in both conditions.

I would use a Wilcoxon test **i**.

ⓔ 2/3 marks awarded g At this point, it becomes a little clearer how this research project will match the requirements of repeated measures design and the research question. It is a shame that it only becomes clear at this point, because marks have been lost for lack of clarity and fit in questions 1 and 2. Certainly, explanation of how the questionnaire will be *scored* should have been in question 2. **h, i** The parts which *are* relevant to this question are the *bottom* line of data (i.e. the totals for same sex versus opposite sex), which gives some sort of overall summary of the results, and the mention of the appropriate test for these data.

(4) This would mean that the data are non-significant.

ⓔ 1/3 marks awarded The student is correct in saying that the data are non-significant but needs to give more detail as to how or why. In these questions, you need to demonstrate an understanding of significance and probability. Therefore, the answer should have referred to $p > 0.05$ indicating that the probability of the data occurring just due to chance factors is *more* than 5%, and said that this is why the hypothesis cannot be accepted and the null should be accepted.

(5) (a) There is no problem with the repeated measures design in this study.

ⓔ 0/3 marks awarded It might be the case that there is no problem with the repeated measures design. However, as it stands, without explaining why and relating it to the study described, this response receives 0 marks. The student should have said: 'This is because, as it is a questionnaire, people just by virtue of their responses are taking part in both conditions (reports of same-sex deception versus reports of opposite-sex deception), so there are no problems with order effects, or with guessing the overall aim of the study and responding to demand characteristics.'

(b) [no answer]

ⓔ 0/3 marks awarded The student has either forgotten to answer this question or else thought that there was no need to because of the response to question (a). Either way, no response means no marks.

(6) This study would have reasonable validity (validity is whether something is measuring what it claims to). **j** This is because we are asking people about their own actual experiences of deception, rather than giving them made-up or false situations (i.e. it has quite good ecological validity). In this way they can write about what actually happened. However, one problem with the validity of this study is that, in a questionnaire, people may not want to reveal the whole truth — perhaps they will not want to admit that they were deceived and so they will not write down all the occasions. In addition, maybe they won't actually remember.

ⓔ 3/3 marks awarded This is quite a good answer — one thing that is always worth doing in such questions is *including a definition* of the term so the examiner is absolutely clear you know what the term means. **j** This student has done this. He also shows understanding that validity has multiple aspects, including ecological validity, and has related these specifically to the investigation described. (The formula to remember for answering such questions is: (i) give general definition, and (ii) relate concept explicitly to own investigation.) There is probably one aspect of the study's validity which has been overlooked: that is whether self-report is the best method overall, for the reason that we may not be able to report all the times we were deceived (as there may have been instances when we never realised we had been deceived). Nevertheless, this is sufficient for full marks because the term is understood, defined and discussed in the context of the investigation with a plausible conclusion.

> **(7)** As I said before, I would tell them what the study was about and ask for their consent.

ⓔ **1/3 marks awarded** A mention is not enough: a much more detailed response is required. The student needs to show understanding of the issue and discuss it in relation to the investigation. Even if this has been said in response to a different question, it should, for safety's sake, be written here too.

ⓔ **Overall, student A receives 18/40 marks for this section.**

> **Student B**

Research question: Can humans accurately judge whether someone is trustworthy from their face?
> **(1)** Participants will make more correct judgements (out of a maximum of 10) **a** about the trustworthiness of persons' faces shown in photographs when the person is genuinely trustworthy **a** than when the person is genuinely untrustworthy **b** (one-tailed) **c**.

ⓔ **3/3 marks awarded** This hypothesis relates clearly and logically to a research question, and is clearly operationalised. **a, b** The IV is 'person trustworthy' and 'person untrustworthy' and the DV is 'correct judgements out of 10'. **c** The hypothesis is correctly one-tailed.

> **(2)** This study will be a repeated measures experimental design because participants will be exposed to both conditions, and these will be under controlled conditions.
> The participants will be an opportunity/quota sample of people from college. For the sake of control, there will be 10 males and 10 females. They will be approached at the end of lessons or during free periods or lunchtime. They will be asked whether they want to take part in a brief experiment about whether or not we are able to recognise trustworthiness from people's faces. If they agree, we will set up an appointment to meet them at a specific time in a specific classroom. Because they know the overall aim of the study and the main details of the study, there is no deception and, in agreeing to take part, they will have given informed consent. When they attend the classroom at the particular time, they will be thanked for coming and we will tell them that they can choose to stop taking part at any time with no pressure (right to withdraw).
> Participants will then be given the specific instructions for the task. They will be asked to look at a series of pictures which will be projected onto a whiteboard using PowerPoint. For each picture, which they will see for exactly 10 seconds (this will

have been programmed into the PowerPoint), they must decide whether the person is/was a trustworthy person or an untrustworthy person who might lie to someone in order, for example, to obtain money. They will be told that a proportion of the pictures (but not exactly what proportion) are of genuinely untrustworthy people. They will be given a photocopied sheet on which to fill in their judgements, as follows:

Participant number	Number of deceptions by same sex	Number of deceptions by opposite sex
1	4	6
2	5	0
3	1	1
4	3	4
Etc.		
Total	19	15

Therefore, they can only choose Trust or Not Trust for each picture. It should also be mentioned that altogether there will be 20 pictures. Of these, 10 will be of people who are renowned for being fraudsters, but whose faces the average sixth-former is not likely to recognise. For instance, there would be a picture of Frank Abagnale, the person whose life the film *Catch Me if You Can* was based on (i.e. someone who is definitely not trustworthy). For each 'fraudster' picture, there would be a non-fraudster picture. This would be matched for sex and time in history (so fashion and photographic look would be quite similar), but there would be nothing in the person's life details to suggest they were untrustworthy, and they certainly would not have made their whole living out of being untrustworthy. This means that altogether there will be 20 photos, 10 of untrustworthy people and 10 of trustworthy people. The order of these will have been randomised, so that there is no specific order (e.g. alternate trustworthy or untrustworthy).

All in all, the participants will see these 20 photos, making their decision on each as they go along. When they reach the end, they will be thanked, asked if they have any questions, and told that, when all the participants have taken part, they will be informed which pictures were actually trustworthy and which were not and also they will be able to see the overall results of the study.

Each participant's results will be scored for which category the picture was in and whether they got their judgement right or wrong. My hypothesis is that they will get more correct judgements for the genuinely trustworthy than the genuinely untrustworthy. Therefore, I will score each response on the response sheet according to whether they were correct or incorrect and count them up according to the category of picture. Thus, the data table will look like this:

Participant number	Number of correct judgements on trustworthy faces	Number of correct judgements on untrustworthy faces
1	8	5
2	5	5
3	7	4
4	9	9
5	5	6
6	2	6
7 etc.	5	2

ⓔ **19/19 marks awarded** This is virtually a perfect answer. For replicability, more than enough detail of the procedure is given (with elaborations) to allow for replication. For fitness of purpose, the study clearly will test the stated hypothesis and research question, has a repeated measures design as required, and poses no ethical or practical problems. For coherence of design, it is clearly and coherently expressed.

(3) To summarise the data, I would calculate the mean, median and mode **d** for each condition (the measures of central tendency) and the range (as a measure of dispersion) **e**. I could present this in a table as follows:

	Correct judgements about trustworthy faces	Correct judgements about untrustworthy faces
Mean	6.7	5.5
Median	6	5
Mode	6	5, 3
Range (top value − bottom value)	7	8

This table will show me, overall, whether there appears to be any difference between the two types of faces, as, in particular, I can compare the means. However, it would not tell me whether the difference is significant or not. For that, I would need to do an inferential test.

The inferential statistical test I would use would be a Wilcoxon test **f** as this is for repeated measures data which are at least ordinal.

ⓔ **3/3 marks awarded** Again, this is an excellent answer. It contains a summary of the results in terms of measures of central tendency and dispersion **d, e**, and **f** the correct inferential test is identified.

(4) A value of $p > 0.05$ means that there is more than 5% probability that the differences in the results occurred due to chance factors, and so we are less than 95% sure that the results occurred because of genuine differences in the data. This means that the results are not significant. As a result, I would have to accept the null hypothesis and reject the experimental hypothesis. Therefore we would conclude that there is no difference in the number of correct judgements (out of a maximum of 10) about the trustworthiness of persons shown in photographs when the person is genuinely trustworthy compared to when the person is genuinely untrustworthy.

ⓔ 3/3 marks awarded This is a full and accurate statement of how to interpret $p > 0.05$, and it is contextualised in terms of the investigation. The student shows very good understanding of probability, significance and decision making in relation to accepting/rejecting hypotheses.

(5) (a) One weakness of the repeated measures design is that, because each participant is taking part in both conditions (looking at both trustworthy pictures and untrustworthy pictures), they have to look at a lot of pictures. This might mean they get 'fatigued' — tired **g** of looking at pictures and making judgements. So they might begin to switch off as they get towards the end of the sequence of pictures and just start guessing or putting down anything, rather than what they really think.

ⓔ 3/3 marks awarded The two obvious weaknesses of repeated measures designs are order effects and fatigue effects. However, the study has already described a way of getting around order effects (randomisation of the order of the pictures). **g** Thus, the student rightly identifies fatigue effects and appropriately applies this to the investigation.

(b) One way to get around this **h** might be to reduce the number of pictures in each condition to 6, so altogether they would look at 12. Another way **i** would be to use a matched pairs design. This would mean having two sets of participants, one group in each condition, but matching them, e.g. for age and sex. Then each participant would only see one set of pictures. However, I think the first way is best.

ⓔ 2/3 marks awarded The student has suggested more than one way. If a student does this, they will be marked for both and then credited with the best answer. In this case, the first answer **h** is not well elaborated and so would only get 1 mark. The second part **i** has more detail, though not enough explanation for full marks.

(6) The validity **j** of this study is OK because they are looking at real pictures of real people. This means the ecological validity **k** is quite high. However, in one way it is quite low. Normally when we look at faces, our understanding of a person comes from how they move their face and eyes — and a photo, which is just still, might be judged in a different way. Also, making judgements very consciously about trustworthiness, as in this experiment, may be different from real life — when perhaps we do it unconsciously because we have to make a decision whether to buy something or let them carry a bag etc.

ⓔ 2/3 marks awarded This is a good response to the question about validity. It is well contextualised. However, **k** it tends to focus only on ecological validity and **j** it has not given a straight definition of validity. On this basis, it only receives 2/3 marks.

Unit G544: Approaches and Research Methods in Psychology

(7) One way of showing awareness of ethical issues concerns the issue of informed consent. Ideally, participants should have a genuine choice of whether to participate or not. If they do participate they should know exactly what they are letting themselves in for and so they should not be deceived in any way or misled about what the study might involve. In this study, the conditions of informed consent are met. This is because the participants are told about the purpose of the study (to find out whether we can accurately judge trustworthiness from faces) and they are also told what the procedure will involve — looking at photos and making judgements. They are not misled in any way about either.

ⓔ **3/3 marks awarded** This answer is excellent, clearly explaining the ethical issue of informed consent and how it is resolved in the study.

ⓔ **Overall, student B receives 38/40 marks for this section.**

Section B

(a) Using your knowledge of psychology, outline the observational method. (4 marks)

ⓔ There is so much to write here. You can define 'observation', mention the different types (controlled, participant etc.) and you can mention event sampling, time sampling, inter-rater reliability etc. You could also mention the type of data that an observation produces.

(b) Describe how the observational method was used in any two pieces of psychological research that you have studied. (8 marks)

ⓔ It is not just a matter of giving two examples here, because the question wants you to state *how* the observational method was actually used.

(c) Giving examples, compare the use of observations with any one other method used in psychology. (12 marks)

ⓔ The important thing to do here is to answer all parts of the question. The first thing is that you must compare observations with another method. This does not mean describe one method and then describe another method — it means that one aspect of observations must be mentioned and then the equivalent for the other method mentioned. An example to illustrate this point must be provided. A second comparison must then be made (this is worth 12 marks), also with relevant examples.

(d) Explain the advantages and disadvantages of the observational method. (8 marks)

ⓔ The question has advantages (plural) and disadvantages (also plural), and as there are 8 marks allocated, there are 2 marks for each. One advantage and one disadvantage will only score a maximum of 4 marks.

(e) Discuss how observational research can help our understanding of everyday life. (8 marks)

ⓔ A discussion gives you the opportunity to show the examiner just how good you are. Take the opportunity. A discussion expects you (for full marks) to have a well-developed set of arguments, that are balanced and coherently organised. You should also have examples to support your points.

Student A

(a) The observational method is where an observer will observe the behaviour of a participant. But this depends on the type of observation. If it is a natural observation **a**, the 'participant' does not know **b** he or she is being observed. This is good because the behaviour is natural and consent isn't needed. But there is no control. If an observation is done in a laboratory **c**, there is control but it isn't a natural environment. The person may be observed through a one-way mirror, to try to get natural behaviour and without the consent of the participant.

ⓔ **2/4 marks awarded a, c** Some of the main components of the observational method are outlined here, as are the different observational methods. However, parts of the answer are rather garbled, and some of it is not strictly accurate (e.g. **b** the point about participants not knowing they are being observed in a natural observation is not always true). Also, it would have been good for the student to say that the observational method itself (rather than observation used as a technique for data collection) involves no manipulation of any independent variable.

(b) I have chosen two core studies because there were no observation studies in my health or crime options.

Observation was used in the study by Bandura. Bandura was a behaviourist who believed that all behaviour is learnt. He wanted to support the theory by showing aggression can be learned. He believed that if a behaviour is observed it will be imitated and if it is not observed then it won't be. He got some children to observe a Bobo doll and some children not to. He then put the children into a room with some toys and observers observed whether the children would copy the aggression or not. There were two observers and they recorded behaviour every 5 seconds. This went on for 20 minutes, so there were 240 observations for each child. **d** As there were two observers, their results were compared. This tests inter-rater reliability. **e** To test reliability the results can be correlated and in the Bandura study the observation correlation was 0.89, which is very good.

Observation was also used in the Piliavin subway Samaritan study. But in this study there was no inter-rater reliability because the two observers were observing different things. One recorded age, sex, race and so on. The other observer recorded specifics of the study such as the time taken for someone to respond. **f** This study was good because participants were in a natural setting where someone could really be ill or drunk, so it was a natural observation. However, as it was a partially controlled field experiment, participants should have given consent, but they did not and they were deceived. These two examples illustrate the strengths and weaknesses of the different types of observations.

ⓔ **5/8 marks awarded** The choice of studies is fine. Using two AS studies has the advantage that you are likely to know these in much greater depth than many A2 studies. The examiner will mark this answer as a whole and not separately for each of the studies, so there can be some trade-off between the quality of the two answers. One of the key things the examiner will look for is the knowledge of detail. **d** The Bandura part contains some detail, such as how often and for how long the observers recorded the behaviour, and the presence of two observers. **f** The Piliavin part contains detail such as what the observers recorded. This is all credit-worthy. However, there are some details which are omitted or mistaken. For example, crucially, for the Bandura study the categories of behaviour are not mentioned at all. Also, for Piliavin it is not specifically mentioned where on a subway the observations took place or what the researchers were watching ('the time taken for someone to respond' does not mention the detail of helping a person who had collapsed). So there is only moderate detail. **e** The examiner will also look for use of terminology (there is some here, used accurately, such as inter-rater reliability). Another important feature is the coherence and structure. It is good to have structured the answer into two parts. However, the answer is not always coherent, and some parts go 'off-track', such as the more evaluative comments towards the end of the section on Piliavin.

(c) Observations are good because if they are natural then participants do not know that they are being observed, as in the Piliavin study. An alternative method is the self-report method. In completing a questionnaire, for example, the person knows they are involved in a study. This means that in one a person 'behaves truthfully' but with a self-report then the person may respond to demand characteristics or give a socially desirable answer. **g** For example, in the study by Dement on sleep, participants could say they were having a dream when they were not, and the 'throwing tomatoes' dream may be made up. Observations give quantitative data **h**, which are numbers, and so statistics can be done and various things can be compared. In Piliavin 62/65 gave spontaneous help in the ill condition. Self-reports can give quantitative data, but often give qualitative data. **i** For example, in Piliavin we know 62/65 helped but because there was no self-report we do not know why **j** people helped or did not help. The two comments made by the ladies were just added anecdotally by one observer; it was not a part of the main study. Observations are used by behaviourists because they give 'hard' scientific data. Self-reports would be rejected by behaviourists. **k** However, self-reports are the domain of the psychodynamic approach, for example Freud. **k**

ⓔ **7/12 marks awarded** The examiner is looking for a good range of evaluative points through comparing observation methods with another method. This student compares observation with self-report, which is a good choice. She makes four points: **g** (i) observation has greater validity because you cannot lie; **h** (ii) observation gives quantitative data (only?) whereas **j** (iii) self-report data can tell you *why*; **i** (iv) observations give hard scientific data, unlike self-report. This is certainly a reasonable range of points, and there are some supporting examples from studies. However, the way in which the points are organised is a little unclear, and sometimes the information is not accurate (e.g. there were more than two comments recorded by the observers in the Piliavin study, and they were, in fact, positively elicited by the observers). **k** The student makes a good reference to different approaches (behaviourist versus psychodynamic), but does not explain or elaborate them sufficiently.

(d) I gave my answer to this question above. But I know if I say 'see above' I won't get any marks, so please be kind Dear Examiner. OK. Explain the advantage. What does this mean? Well, an advantage is something good, and the more good things that happen the better it is, and things are more likely to be accepted. On the other hand if something has lots of disadvantages then something won't be accepted and that will be that. **l**

Does this mean that my answer to the above question (c) was wrong? The advantages of the observational method are: it can be natural; it can give quantitative data; often participants do not need to give consent. The disadvantages are that it does not give qualitative data, so gives no reasons why a behaviour occurs. Natural observations cannot be controlled. Another advantage is that if there are two observers then inter-rater reliability can be used to test the agreement. But a disadvantage is that if there is only one observer, who is to say that the one observer is not biasing the observation. **m**

ⓔ **2/8 marks awarded** Yes, there is some danger of repetition in these series of questions. This is another reason why it is a good idea to plan your answers. **l** The first paragraph is weak and waffly. **m** The second paragraph makes some relatively sound points, but without elaboration — it is quite list-like and has not really *explained* as the question instructed. Even the second band requires some elaboration, so this answer is limited to the bottom band.

(e) Observations can help our understanding of everyday life in many ways. If behaviour is done in a laboratory people know they are in a study and so may respond to demand characteristics. They often complete an artificial task; they have been reduced to isolate the IV. This is reductionism and it is also the experimental method. Yes, this is good, but it does not tell us very much about behaviour in everyday life. If we can observe natural behaviour then we can see how people really behave when they are not in a lab, when they are not reduced and when they are not doing some completely artificial task. We might be able to learn things in a lab, such as how obedient people are (i.e. Milgram), but real-life examples of this are much better. The Hofling study is a good example, but the 'hoax most cruel' story where a McDonald's manager stripped a girl tells us about real life. The video of this is on YouTube, showing that a lot of our everyday life behaviour is on CCTV. This means that we are individuated rather than deindividuated. Newman says individuating is a good thing whereas Zimbardo says that people behave antisocially when they are deindividuated. This is why criminals often wear hoodies. But this is often not true because I wear a hoody and I'm not a criminal. So observation can help but not with true understanding. Using my example earlier, just because we know 62/65 people helped in the Piliavin study we do not know why they did. So observation has a really big weakness. It gives us data, but it doesn't tell us why and so we can only guess why. Thinking about it, Piliavin came up with cost–benefit to explain why people helped or did not help, but Piliavin didn't ask any of the participants why. Maybe Piliavin already had the answer as to why people helped, or just guessed. So observations help to a certain extent, but to get a full picture or full understanding we need to use a range of methods.

e **4/8 marks awarded** This is quite a difficult question. The student has had a reasonable stab at it and makes some sound points about observation and everyday life; there is also an attempt at balance (i.e. a mixture of good and bad points). The main thing that lets this student down is the organisational/coherence aspect of the response.

e **Overall, student A receives 20/40 marks for this section.**

Student B

(a) The observational method, unsurprisingly, involves observing participants. While there are several different types of observational method (controlled, naturalistic, participant) **a**, the main feature of a pure observational method is that it does not involve any manipulation of an independent variable (IV). Participants are observed, and this might be an unstructured observation (all behaviour is noted) or a structured observation (specific categories are decided beforehand and noted down). Also, an observation can be made systematic by either adopting event sampling (noting down every time a particular thing happens) or time sampling **b** (noting down what is happening every *x* seconds or minutes, on a set time interval). Finally, the observational method can make use of recording equipment such as tape recording equipment or CCTV.

e **4/4 marks awarded** This answer is excellent. The observational method is clearly and accurately described, with no errors and sound use of terminology. For example, **a** the student refers to three types of observations and **b** refers to both event and time sampling.

(b) One study which uses the observational method is Savage-Rumbaugh et al.'s study of chimpanzees. **c** This study looks at the extent to which chimpanzees can learn symbolic language. The main participant was a pygmy chimpanzee called Kanzi who was brought up using 'lexigrams' with a lot of human contact. Observation was used to record *all* of Kanzi's utterances between the ages of 30 and 47 months. When indoors, Kanzi could use a computer with a touch screen and so the utterance was automatically 'observed' and recorded. Outside, Kanzi touched a board and these utterances were observed and written down by the observer. Alongside this, each utterance was also coded according to the context that Kanzi made it in — so as well as whether it was correct or incorrect, they also noted whether it was spontaneous (Kanzi used the word with no cueing from the researchers), and whether it was in response to a particular question or request. The researchers established the reliability of observations by comparing a video tape of 4.5 hours of observations with the observational records that were made at the time of the same 4.5 hours. They found a very high degree of reliability, with only one disagreement about spontaneity.

Another study which uses observation is Piliavin. **d** Although this is a field experiment, the data collection uses observation. There were two observers, always female, and, sitting in the 'critical area' in the carriage where the stooge collapsed, they noted details of the passengers on the carriage (number, sex, ethnicity), who helped (sex and ethnicity), latency of helping, and whether additional helpers also helped after the first person, and they noted down other responses to the emergency situation, such as whether people left the carriage, or people said anything about the situation (either spontaneously or because the observer tried to get them to say something). These observations were carried out over 102 trials.

e **8/8 marks awarded c, d** This answer considers two studies, which are accurately and coherently described with sufficient detail and elaboration. The quality of communication is also high, so the answer merits a top-band mark.

(c) I am going to compare observations with self-report. Observations are particularly good for investigating how people *actually* behave, rather than how they *say* they might behave. **e** One everyday example of this is in sleep research, where insomniacs often report not having slept at all during the night, but when observed are seen to get more sleep than they report. An example of this in a psychological study is probably Piliavin. In this case, the observations showed that there was a high degree of helping overall in that the stooge was usually helped. However, quite a lot of people on the train did not offer help, and first helpers were more likely to be men than women. It is unlikely that these results would have been obtained using self-report because people in questionnaires will want to give socially desirable answers, or say they would help even if they don't know what they would actually do when faced with an emergency situation. Therefore, observations are likely to give more valid results than self-report.

The use of observations, in comparison with self-report, though, is much more intensive and time-consuming for researchers. For example, in trying to measure adherence of patients to medical requests, such as taking medicine, it is clear that simply asking patients (e.g. in an online questionnaire, or when they revisit their doctor) will be a fairly rapid and easy way to collect data from a decent sample. However, observing people and whether or not they take every pill would be very time-intensive in order to get a decent size of sample of people.

This leads me to another issue. Observations can have more issues around ethics **f** in terms of privacy. This is because, with a self-report, respondents might just choose to skip a question which they think is a bit intrusive or they do not want to answer. However, with an observation, participants may not even know they are being observed. The current ethical guidelines are that, if the observation is taking place in a public space, the researchers need not seek informed consent, on the basis that participants know their behaviour might be observed by anyone in any case. However, some participants may feel that they might have wanted to give consent or have some knowledge of being observed. And, in some cases, it may be that parents or teachers consent on behalf of students to be observed. For example, in some of the research on Aronson's Jigsaw Learning technique (from the Education unit), some participants in the classrooms may have felt that the presence of an observer made them uncomfortable as they would feel monitored and judged while going about their daily life.

Observation, although used right across psychology, is perhaps the method most suited to the behaviourist perspective. **g** This is because behaviourists reject the study of the mind exactly because it cannot be directly observed and so people can only make inferences or even just 'guesses' about how it really works. According to hard behaviourists, only actions etc. which are directly observable should be the subject of psychological investigation — and so observation is really at the heart of behaviourism and its scientific agenda. This is probably one reason why observation is the main data collection method in Bandura's Bobo doll study. In comparison, self-report would be rejected by behaviourists. This is because self-report relies heavily on what people *think* rather than how they behave. Interestingly, self-report is one of the favoured methods of the psychodynamic approach, since much of this involves patients, in therapy, reporting their dreams and personal experiences (e.g. Freud's Little Hans study).

e 12/12 marks awarded This answer contains a range of points on a variety of topics, such as **e** method, **f** ethics and **g** approach. Each point is clearly explained, with some examples, and shows quite a sophisticated understanding of observational research and the issues around it. From this answer, the examiner is left in no doubt that this student really understands psychology. The mark scheme for top band requires that 'the quality of argument arising from points is clear and well developed' — and this is certainly a feature of this answer.

(d) One advantage **h** of the observational method is that it has reasonably good validity. This is because observations are particularly good for investigating how people *actually* behave, rather than how they *say* they might behave. One everyday example of this is in sleep research, where insomniacs often report not having slept at all during the night, but when observed are seen to get more sleep than they report. An example of this in a psychological study is probably Piliavin. In this case, the observations showed that there was a high degree of helping overall in that the stooge was usually helped. However, quite a lot of people on the train did not offer help, and the first helpers were more likely to be men than women. It is unlikely that these results would have been obtained using self-report, because people in questionnaires will want to give socially desirable answers, or say they would help even if they don't know what they would actually do when faced with an emergency situation. Therefore, observations are likely to give more valid results than self-report.

Another advantage of observations **i**, especially naturalistic and participant observations, is that they can collect information which is high in ecological validity. This is because they involve observing people in their natural environment going about their natural lives. This is in sharp contrast to a laboratory experiment, where the environment will be artificial and alien (and bound to influence behaviour), and the task is likely to be something also unnatural and artificial, for example a word memory test, which bears little resemblance to any authentic memory task.

One disadvantage **j** of observations is that they are highly work-intensive. For each person in the sample, the observation might take quite a long time and be quite intense. For example, in Bandura, they observed each child for 20 minutes and noted down which type of behaviour occurred every 5 seconds — totalling 240 observations per participant. This requires a lot of concentration, and the ability to categorise the behaviour quickly and note it down quickly. Of course, if the behaviour is filmed on CCTV, this takes some of the immediate pressure off coding 'live' behaviour — however, it is still very intensive and time-consuming. This leads on to another disadvantage **k**: because of the complexity of coding behaviour, it is quite easy to make errors. This can lead to observations which have low reliability. Interestingly, in Savage-Rumbaugh's study, one block of 4.5 hours of Kanzi's behaviour was coded twice — once 'live', as it happened, and once from a video. There was quite a lot of agreement about Kanzi's utterances in terms of being correct. However, there was one disagreement over whether one utterance was imitated or not, and also the coding from the video picked up several extra utterances which had not been noticed in the 'live' coding.

ⓔ **8/8 marks awarded** This answer is well structured and organised, as well as accurate. It identifies **h, i** two advantages and **j, k** two disadvantages and they are each well developed. There is some overlap of material between the answers to question parts (d) and (c); however, this is, if anything, the fault of the question, and so the student is probably justified in repeating some of the material.

(e) Observational research is very good for understanding everyday life, for the main reason that it is a research technique suited to ecologically valid (i.e. natural) situations. **l** For example, Hofling's study, which included observation, found out how nurses respond to orders from doctors. This tells us a lot about unquestioning obedience, especially in a situation where hierarchy is already determined. It indicates that people in other jobs may well act on orders from a line manager even when they may logically know that this is not the best thing to do. This is an example of how observational research can tell you about everyday life.

However, there are some things that observations are not so good at. **m** For example, if you want to find out how stressed someone is, observing them is probably not the best way as people can feel quite deeply stressed but keep it quite well hidden and only reveal it in private. So, in this case, a self-report questionnaire like Holmes and Rahe would be able to tell us more about stress and everyday life. Thus, observations are good for behaviours etc. which are actually *visible* but are limited when it comes to private behaviours or mental processes which cannot be directly observed.

ⓔ **5/8 marks awarded** This answer is well focused on the usefulness of observational research to understanding everyday life (and not just psychology in general). The points made are quite full and meaningful. **l, m** However, only two points have been made and this prevents the answer from reaching the top band.

ⓔ **Overall, student B receives 37/40 marks for this section — a clear A grade.**

Knowledge check answers

1 One similarity is that they are both experiments (with IV, controls and DV). One difference is the setting: one is done in a laboratory and the other is done in a much more natural environment.

2 'Controlled conditions' means somewhere that is kept the same for all participants and that is not where you would naturally come across the particular behaviour you are investigating. It could be a laboratory, a clinical room, or someone's office borrowed as a quiet place to conduct your experiment.

3 The studies by Baron-Cohen et al., Loftus and Palmer, Bandura et al., Dement and Kleitman, Maguire et al., and Sperry.

4 The study by Piliavin et al. is the most obvious example of a field experiment.

5 In a laboratory or field experiment, the researcher manipulates the IV. That is, he or she makes the conditions happen or decides who is in which group. He or she can then measure the effects (the DV). In a natural experiment, the IV varies naturally, without the researcher's intervention.

6 (a) In a structured interview, each participant is asked exactly the same questions in the same order. In an unstructured interview, the researcher asks different questions, depending on where the discussion takes him or her. (b) There are different kinds of questions that you could include in any self-report measure. Closed questions usually have a limited range of answers, while open questions allow a free response.

7 The study by Bandura et al. used controlled observation. The room in which they observed the children (the test room) had the same layout and the same toys for each child. The study by Rosenhan was a participant observation because Rosenhan was a pseudo-patient, i.e. he pretended to be a real patient and took observations of the participants.

8 One disadvantage of conducting a study in a laboratory is that it is low in ecological validity. The setting is artificial as the participants are travelling there and the task they are required to do may also be something they would never normally do in real life.

9 One advantage of conducting a field experiment is that it may be higher in ecological validity than a laboratory experiment.

10 One advantage of an observation is that the observed behaviour is natural and can be measured objectively. In the study by Piliavin et al., participants did not know they were in a study and so responded as they would have done normally. A disadvantage of an observation is that participants cannot explain why they behaved in a particular way. In the study by Piliavin et al., participants could not say why they behaved as they did. If they had been asked, they might have been upset when realising they had been deceived.

11 There will be a significant difference in the number of Zener cards correctly guessed out of 20 between participants who are 'sheep' and those who are 'goats'.

12 The core study by Milgram. The study by Thigpen and Cleckley, or the prison simulation study by Haney, Banks and Zimbardo.

13 Ordinal data will simply be the order in which participants finish a race. Someone will be first, then someone else second, then third etc.

14 With ordinal data, we could say that a rating of 6 was more than a rating of 5, but we could not be sure that the difference between 5 and 6 meant the same as the difference between 7 and 8. However, with interval level data, the points are evenly spaced: the intervals between them are equal. To take an everyday example, the difference between 35°C and 40°C is the same as the difference between 20°C and 25°C.

15 There is less than 5% probability that differences between the two sets of scores occurred due to chance factors alone. That is, there is more than 95% probability that the results occurred due to a real difference between the two conditions.

16 This means that, if the level of significance has been set at 0.05 to avoid type 1 and type 2 errors, the hypothesis would be accepted and the null hypothesis rejected.

17 A type 2 error is when we reject the alternate hypothesis and accept the null hypothesis when actually the alternate hypothesis was true — a false negative.

18 A Wilcoxon test.

19 This is used when you are looking for (a) a difference between (b) two conditions. (c) It is for ordinal data (or interval data if necessary) and (d) an independent measures design.

20 This is the part of psychology which genuinely engages in how we think. Many people regard this topic area as central to psychology. One example would be from the study by Yochelson and Samenow (1976), who found that criminals thought differently from non-criminals. Altogether, Yochelson and Samenow found 52 thinking patterns.

21 Often, physiological research shows only an association between a psychological event and a biological event as we do not know the direction of cause (i.e. which event caused the other). For example, in the case of Dement and Kleitman, we do not know whether dreaming caused the changes in EEG patterns, or if the changes in the brain waves caused the dreaming — or if something else (e.g. activity in a specific part of the brain) caused both things to happen together. A fair amount of physiological research faces this type of problem. An example from A2 is the study by Raine et al. on the brain scans of murderers. Did the abnormalities in the brain cause them to murder, or did the murder create the abnormalities in the brain? As with the AS example, any correlation does not show cause and effect.

22 One assumption is that in any group of people, there are differences between those people in terms of their personal qualities, the ways in which they respond to situations etc. Any study may generalise but it will not apply to all people all of the time because there are always individual differences.

23 This approach emphasises growth and change and how an experience at one point in life can have various consequences at later stages. It helps us to understand how children behave at various stages in their early life. For example, little Hans progressed through a number of developmental stages, and at

the time of the study was said to be in the phallic stage, having progressed through the oral and anal stages.

24 An assumption of the social approach is that we can only understand people in the context of how they operate in their interactions and perceptions of others. Why does someone behave in a particular way in a particular situation? We only know by looking at the context of the people around them.

25 Because behaviourism refuses to acknowledge how we think, how we make sense of the world, some explanations it provides are incomplete. Consider, for example, the study by DiNardo et al. (1988) in which two people who are bitten by a dog. One develops a dog phobia and one does not. Why? It is probably because of the differing ways in which they make sense of the situation, the cognitions they have about the dog and other dogs. Behaviourism fails to account for this.

26 Freud proposed a theory of psychosexual development, describing a number of stages which every child progressed. According to Freud, each stage has a particular (predetermined) focus of 'sexual gratification' and it is important that the conflict is resolved so that the child can continue into adulthood without any dysfunctional behaviour. The stages begin with the oral stage (age 0–1), with the focus on sucking and later biting, moving on to the anal stage (age 1–3), with the focus on expelling and retaining faeces.

27 The study by Bandura et al. on learning aggression is an example of environmental determinism. They believe that all behaviour is learnt and so the environment in which this takes place is crucial. The medical or biological explanation of mental disorders believes in biological determinism, holding the view that disorders are due to either inherited factors or chemical imbalances.

28 The nature view believes that all behaviour is genetically (biologically) determined. The nurture view believes that behaviour is learnt. This means that all human behaviour, however complex it might be, can be reduced to nothing more than say learning. For behaviourists, this is nothing more than classical and operant conditioning and observational learning.

29 The nature view believes that all behaviour is genetically (biologically) determined. The nurture view believes that behaviour is mainly, or entirely, acquired through experience and the influence of the environment is crucial. This is environmental determinism.

30 On one hand, psychology uses the scientific method: it is carried out through genuine experimentation (manipulation of IVs), using many controls. Hypotheses can be tested empirically, so that theories are tested and refined and so knowledge progresses. On the other hand, psychology's subject matter is humans. They cannot be investigated in the same way as, say, chemistry or physics because the mind, motivation, emotion and so on are not open to genuine scientific and empirical research since they are not actually observable.

31 An individual or dispositional explanation for behaviour will look to some feature or characteristic within the person rather than caused by the situation.

The study by Rosenhan shows that mental illness was perceived because of the situation and context. Thus, normal behaviour, e.g. waiting at the canteen, was seen as 'oral acquisitive behaviour' — a situational explanation.

From the forensic option, the work by Lombroso suggested that various criminal types were based upon physical characteristics. These physical anomalies included the size or shape of the ears, the length of the nose and arms, the symmetry of the face and the amount of facial hair — a dispositional explanation.

32 To be useful, any study (a) should be ethical — participants should give informed consent and not be deceived (however, a study may need to be unethical to be really useful); (b) should be ecologically valid — studies conducted in a laboratory may not be useful as they are low in ecological validity; (c) should use a representative sample and be generalisable; (d) should apply worldwide, so there should be no ethnocentrism.

33 A longitudinal study takes place over a period of time, usually following one or more participants throughout the period (or visiting them at regular intervals) to monitor changes.

One problem is that it can be difficult to track participants over a long period of time — for example, they may move house or may not want to continue participating. Thus, longitudinal studies tend to lose participants as they go along. This is called 'participant attrition'.

One example is the study by Freud on Little Hans and a second is the study by Thigpen and Cleckley on Eve. Neither participant withdrew, with Eve being studied over at least 14 months and Little Hans for a number of years.

34 (a) Quantitative data will allow the calculation of measures of central tendency and dispersion (mean, median, mode and range). (b) Quantitative data allow statistics to be applied and so marks can be gained for stating what test would be applied and why. (c) Quantitative data allow acceptance or rejection of hypotheses through significance levels.

35 Qualitative data can help us understand why people behave in a particular way. For example in the study by Piliavin et al. on subway Samaritans, no qualitative data were gathered. This meant that as they did not ask anyone why they helped or did not help, they could only assume people behaved according to the model of arousal and cost/benefit.

36 Qualitative data are in the form of words. Examples include descriptions of events, quotes from participants, or descriptions of participants' responses to a task. Qualitative data can help us understand why people behave in a particular way.